ELGAR AS I KNEW HIM

ELGAR WITH THE AUTHOR WALKING BY THE SEVERN

From a snapshot taken by Mr. E. Hall, Principal Trumpeter of the B.B.C. Orchestra

ELGAR AS I KNEW HIM

By

WILLIAM H. REED

LONDON

VICTOR GOLLANCZ LTD

1936

First published September 1936
Second impression October 1936

Printed in Great Britain by
The Camelot Press Ltd., London and Southampton

TO ALL ELGAR'S FRIENDS
AND LOVERS OF HIS MUSIC

But a book is written, not to multiply the voice merely, not to carry it merely, but to perpetuate it.

The author has something to say which he perceives to be true and useful, or helpfully beautiful. So far as he knows, no one has said it; so far as he knows, no one else can say it.

He is bound to say it, clearly and melodiously if he may; clearly at all events.

CONTENTS

9

LIST OF ILLUSTRATIONS

PREFACE

AT THE INSTANCE of Mr. Bernard Shaw, and many others of the friends and admirers of Sir Edward Elgar, I have been persuaded—I might almost say cajoled—into setting down these intimate and personal things concerning him, gathered during a close friendship extending over a period of nearly thirty years.

I was very diffident about undertaking this task, knowing full well that there are many others possessed of literary ability and experience in writing who are far better qualified in that respect. It is one thing to tell these intimate anecdotes and happenings at the dinner-table or in ordinary conversation, and quite another to set them down in readable form to be perused in cold blood by the multitude.

It was pointed out to me, however, that I was probably the only person who had the close knowledge of these daily happenings, and the only person, therefore, who could set them down at first hand. I was flattered by being told that my memory was so good that I could repeat Elgar's exact words in recounting any of these anecdotes, just as if he had made the remarks recorded in this book yesterday; but I knew very well that, if I did not make this effort

13

soon, I should forget a good deal of it; in which case, most, if not all, of these otherwise unobtainable details of his life would be lost.

While still hesitating and turning the matter over in my mind, recalling the past, and testing my memory concerning these things, I received a letter from Mr. Bernard Shaw calculated to fire me with the necessary courage to make a start:

"SCHEME FOR THE ELGAR BOOK
SECTION ONE
PERSONAL

"Jump straight into the story at once—thus, 'Elgar and I met first in 19?? '," etc.

This was followed by another letter:

" Perhaps I should get the enclosed typed for you; but, as all orchestral players are inured to impossible manuscripts, I send it, to save time, just as I scrawled it. It may just serve to start you. Once started, you will have no difficulty in going ahead in your own way."

Thus stimulated, I hastened to begin.

After writing some ten or twelve pages I sent the sheets over to Malvern, where Bernard Shaw was residing. His reply was:

" This is all right. Carry on like that and the book will be a success. I read it to T. E. Shaw

(Col. Lawrence of Arabia), who has a very keen literary flair, and to Mrs. Shaw. They agreed with me without a moment's hesitation."

After reading this, and being further assured verbally that, though playing the fiddle requires a high degree of trained professional skill, literature is successfully practised every day by cheerful amateurs, I threw modesty to the winds and went ahead recklessly.

All the occurrences, episodes, and anecdotes recorded in this book are the things Elgar told me in daily conversation, or things I witnessed, or in which I took part. I have rejected all suppositions and hearsay, with the exception of the description of the Opera, upon which he was engaged when he died. For this description I am indebted to Sir Barry Jackson, who was, in fact, helping Elgar with the libretto and with his advice; so I shall give it, with Sir Barry's permission, in his own words.

In Part II, " Elgar the Composer," I have avoided any technical discussion of his works, and have, I hope, steered clear of comparisons, either with the works of his contemporaries or with the great masters. Comparisons of this sort seem futile; one might as well compare oak-trees with elms, or beeches with chestnuts, as seek to appraise the worth of one great master by comparison with the work of another.

I have had to stint myself in musical illustration as far as possible; for, if I were to let myself go, there would be more music than words in the book. So I have confined myself to quoting the reference numbers which are to be found in all the published copies of the works of Elgar, so as to facilitate quick identification of the bar or bars under discussion. I have made no attempt to deal with his works in any sort of chronological order: they have been surveyed as a whole and dipped into here and there merely to illustrate points.

In Part III, " The Third Symphony," I quote a letter Bernard Shaw wrote me on the subject of any attempt to complete this Unfinished Symphony. All the attempts to complete the Venus of Milo with a pair of arms have failed. In Elgar's case, we have the arms without the statue: a much more insoluble problem.

I have to record the good offices of the British Broadcasting Corporation in allowing me to make use of the photostat copies of the extracts from the original MSS. of the Third Symphony as left by Sir Edward Elgar. Without the rare cultured spirit and fine personal feeling of Sir John Reith, as director of that great institution, the symphony would never have been begun.

My thanks are due to all those who have helped me in the task of compiling this book. To Mrs. Blake (Carice Elgar) for her unfailing interest and the trouble she has taken to verify any of the facts or the dates of events as recorded. To my friend Irene

Collins, M.A., for her help in punctuation: an art terrifying to one accustomed to the precision of musical notation.

Thus helped and encouraged, I send forth this volume with the hope that its perusal may bring happy memories to those who had the good fortune to know Elgar; that it may prove illuminating for those who had not that good fortune; and that it may play its small part in helping to perpetuate the love and esteem felt by so many for Sir Edward Elgar, his genius, and his works.

PART I

PERSONAL

PERSONAL

THE FIRST TIME I had the opportunity of speaking
to Elgar was at a Promenade Concert rehearsal at
Queen's Hall in 1902. We had been rehearsing his
funeral march from *Diarmid and Grania,* and I was so
thrilled by the music, and by what was to my ear the
newness of the orchestral sound, that I left my seat
among the first violins and followed him out through
the curtains until I caught him up half way up the
stairs. Breathlessly I begged him to excuse me for
thrusting myself forward, but I was anxious to know
whether he gave lessons in harmony, counterpoint,
etc. His answer was characteristic: " My dear boy
I don't know anything about those things." Rather
subdued, I returned to my seat in the orchestra,
hoping that Mr. Wood (now Sir Henry) had not
noticed my brief absence. Little did I then think that
those few words exchanged on the stairs at Queen's
Hall were to be the prelude to a firm and most intimate friendship, which would last without any break
for over thirty years: in fact, until the day of his death.

It was soon very evident that Elgar was not annoyed
by my temerity in running after him that day, for
afterwards, whenever he came to conduct, he never

failed to speak to me on his way to or from the conductor's desk, always finding something friendly and encouraging to say. Naturally very much flattered that he should remember my existence, what was my astonishment when, meeting him one day in Regent Street, he stopped me to know whether I had any spare time, and if so could I come up to see him at a flat in New Cavendish Street where he was then living. He was sketching out something for the fiddle, and wanted to settle, in his own mind, some question of bowing and certain intricacies in the passage-work. As can easily be imagined, I leapt at his suggestion.

It was at the flat in New Cavendish Street that I was introduced to Lady Elgar. She, in my opinion, exercised a decisive influence upon Elgar and his music. She had the loftiest ideals imaginable, and, though not able to criticise him technically, she had unerring judgment and æsthetic sense, amounting to a sure instinct for the rightness and fitness of things. One evening later in the year, Elgar had been working nearly all day; and we were sitting discussing the details of the construction and the possible lay-out of the orchestration which would follow, when he suddenly said, " You know, Billy "—I was Billy by this time—"my wife is a wonderful woman. I play phrases and tunes to her because she always likes to see what progress I have been making. Well, she nods her head and says nothing, or just ' Oh, Edward ! '—but I

know whether she approves or not, and I always feel
that there is something wrong with it if she doesn't.
She never expresses her disapproval, as she feels she
is not sufficiently competent to judge of the workings
of the musical mind; but, a few nights before you
came, we were at Plas Gwyn, Hereford. I played some
of the music I had written that day, and she nodded
her head appreciatively, except over one passage, at
which she sat up, rather grimly, I thought. However,
I went to bed leaving it as it was; but I got up as soon
as it was light and went down to look over what I had
written. I found it as I had left it, except that there
was a little piece of paper, pinned over the offending
bars, on which was written, ' All of it is beautiful and
just right, except this ending. Don't you think, dear
Edward, that this end is just a little . . . ?' Well, Billy,
I scrapped that end. Not a word was ever said about
it; but I rewrote it; and as I heard no more I knew
that it was approved."

When I arrived at the New Cavendish Street flat
on my first visit, one morning about ten o'clock, I
found E. striding about with a lot of loose sheets of
music paper, arranging them in different parts of the
room. Some were already pinned on the backs of
chairs, or stuck up on the mantelpiece ready for me
to play. After my introduction to Lady Elgar, we
started work without losing a moment. What we
played was a sketchy version of the Violin Concerto.
He had got the main ideas written out, and, as he

23

put it, " japed them up " to make a coherent piece.
I understood him to say that he had started the concerto some little time before, and that Lady Speyer—
an accomplished violinist, wife of Sir Edgar Speyer,
and known on the concert platform as Madame von
Stosch—had played it over with him. Dissatisfied with
it, he had put it on one side for a while, but had
suddenly seen it all in a new light, and now, though
using the same themes, was treating them in a new
manner, besides introducing new material.

This morning's work was a unique experience to
me: it gave me a very intimate view of Elgar as a
composer, revealing the singularity of his mental
processes, the originality of his methods, and the
surprising speed at which he worked.

More visits to New Cavendish Street followed; and
the discussion and analysis of the concerto as it grew
were to me a great joy and indeed an education. He
was always very diffident; but he knew when anything he had written gave him pleasure. There was
no false modesty about his joy in hearing the solo
violin boldly entering in the first movement (Fig. 9)
with the *concluding* half of the principal subject instead
of with the beginning, as if answering a question
instead of stating a fact. Several times we played that
opening, to his infinite glee at the novelty of the idea.
He has often said to me, " If you have a good idea,
don't waste it: make the most of it." At the beginning of the development section (Fig. 27), after the

big *tutti*, the violin enters on the second half of the phrase *fortissimo* against the *piano* and *pianissimo* of the orchestra. In fact, the solo violin never plays the opening statement throughout the concerto; even in the Cadenza of the last movement it enters sadly and wistfully at the third bar after the tenderest expression of the first two bars by the orchestra. And so, too, at the end of the Cadenza (Fig. 107).

It will be noticed that at each one of these repetitions there is always a subtle difference, either of character, expression, or nuance: in a word, of the " lighting." The treatment at the end of the big *tutti* before Fig. 27 is turbulent and angry; and the entrance of the soloist has a calming effect, forming a link between the agitation of the *tutti* and the tranquillity which follows. The subdued *mezzo voce* of the opening of the Cadenza, and the introduction of the pauses at the end—as though he were loth to leave this theme—are typical examples of his capacity for imposing every change of mood on the same notes. If we compare the gentle first phrase of the second subject (at Fig. 16) with its developments and variations, notably in the *tutti* which follows at Fig. 24, where it assumes quite a pompous manner, we get another glimpse of the way his mind worked in shaping and developing his thematic material, and quite another light is thrown upon it at (34), where we pass from *grandioso* to an animated and expressive dialogue between the solo violin and its orchestral

25

companions. He would write a phrase many times with a slight alteration in each version, or make such drastic harmonic or rhythmic changes as to alter the entire character of the theme as originally conceived. He loved to present his ideas in all moods and then consider them from every aspect. It was never too much trouble to write a passage again and yet again, if he were not satisfied with it, or if, with his characteristic restlessness, he had started a new hare.

Soon the time arrived when the flat had to be given up, and Sir Edward went to stay at Bray near Maidenhead, at a house called The Hut, belonging to Mr. Leo Schuster: Frankie, as Elgar and the other frequenters of The Hut always called him.

It was not very long before I received an urgent summons to go there. The slow movement and the first movement of the concerto were almost finished; and the Coda was ready. Could I, therefore, come and play them with him? I went on the following Sunday. Many years afterwards the house was re-named The Long White Cloud, presumably by a New Zealand proprietor; but I prefer to remember it by the name it bore when I played so much music there with Sir Edward, and where he told me so much about himself and his early struggles.

I can see it now as it looked that spring morning when I first arrived. It was a sweet riverside house, raised several feet above the level of the lawn, with wooden steps leading up to the verandah from the

PLATE I : ELGAR THE CHEMIST WORKING IN HIS LABORATORY
KNOWN AS " THE ARK " AT HEREFORD

gravel path. It was evidently constructed in anticipation of floods, being only a stone's throw from the Thames, which, however, flowed past serenely enough between its banks whenever I happened to be there. Across the lawn, and almost screened by trees, was the studio, away from the house and approached by stones placed in the grass about a pace apart. It had rather a barn-like exterior, but, inside, it was a home for most of the curios, Chinese ornaments, rare and extraordinary objects which Frankie had collected and brought home from all parts of the world. I remember particularly well a stuffed lizard, or a member of that genus—a fine specimen, though perhaps rather large for a lizard. It was suspended from the ceiling in such a way as to be swayed by every gust of wind coming in through door or window, and I always felt that it swung round to have a good look at us when we played the slow movement or the opening of the Finale, for it was here that this first took shape.

In the course of my visits I met many of the Elgar worshippers who surrounded him in those days: Mrs. Stuart-Wortley (afterwards Lady Stuart of Wortley), Lalla Vandervelde (wife of the Belgian Socialist Minister, and daughter of Mr. Edward Speyer of Shenley, a notable music-lover), and many others. They all seemed a very happy party, each going his own way and meeting on the raised verandah for meals. Sir Edward spent most of his time at work in the studio, where the others wisely left him alone unless invited to come and hear some of the concerto if I happened to be staying there. When we were tired of playing, or if Sir Edward wanted to go out in the air for a change, the fiddle was laid in its case and we went off together, strolling about the river-bank, watching the small fish in the water and enjoying the quiet beauty of the place. During these walks he took me more and more into his confidence, until to my great joy I found myself gradually becoming one of his intimate friends.

Soon after these visits to Bray, Sir Edward returned to his home in Hereford, Plas Gwyn, where he became very busy with the Finale of the concerto. He had arrived at the point where he had an inspiration for a somewhat elaborate Cadenza, to be carried out in a new manner, and therefore calling for my experimental help. It was to sum up all the principal ideas in the concerto; and it would be accompanied! This was a staggering novelty: whoever heard of an accompanied Cadenza in a concerto? Certainly I had not; so off I went to Hereford. On arriving at the house I found the studio in the state I had become accustomed to at the London flat: music-paper all over the room, scraps at any vantage point, many different versions of the same thing with the different bowings to be tried for each. At once we plunged into it. Passages were tried in different ways: the notes were regrouped or the phrasing altered. The Cadenza was in pieces; but soon the parts took shape and were knit together to become an integral part of the concerto. Ivor Atkins, the organist of Worcester Cathedral (now Sir Ivor Atkins), came and played the piano accompaniment, while Sir Edward strode about the room, listening and rubbing his hands excitedly. He would dash up to us with a pencil and scratch something out, writing an alternative in the margin, or add an "*allargando*" or "*tenuto*" over a certain note to make it stand out: always trying every possible effect in tone gradation, slurred or detached bowing, harmonics or natural notes.

He was untiring in his efforts to explore all the possibilities in his music, and bubbling over with enthusiasm when the quest was ended and he had found what he had been seeking.

The concerto was finished during the summer. That being the year (1910) when the Three Choirs held their Festival at Gloucester, I went to the house of my old friend Herbert Brewer on the Saturday following the London rehearsals. At once I knew that something exciting was afoot, because Sir Edward had been in twice to see if I had arrived.

At all the Festivals of the Three Choirs it was customary for Sir Edward to take a house for the week and have a house-party of music-lovers. On this occasion he had taken one in College Green, a house normally used for the cookery school. It had a very large room containing a grand piano and several pictures. What these represented I never discovered, as they all had their faces turned to the wall. In many of the houses that Sir Edward had lent to him, or that he had taken for a short period (furnished), the pictures were either turned round the wrong way or covered over with some hanging material—even newspaper. No comment was ever made about the odd effect produced in the room. He just didn't want these family portraits, or whatever they were, staring at him; so he turned them round or covered them up.

As soon as I heard I was wanted, I quickly found Sir Edward and learned that Frank Schuster had made a grand suggestion, which was: to invite a select number of people to come to that nice large room at the cookery school on the Sunday evening, when we—Sir Edward and I—could play them the Violin Concerto right through. I said it was an excellent idea, although I must confess I had some inward qualms. I knew every note of the concerto, and exactly how he liked it played: every nuance, every shade of expression; yet I felt a little overwhelmed at being asked to play the solo part at what would actually be the very first performance before an audience. It was one of those facts that you cannot annihilate by just calling it private.

When the time arrived I went over to the house and found the guests assembled. Nearly all the prominent musicians engaged at the Festival were there: the three Festival conductors, Sinclair, Atkins, and Brewer; the past organists of Gloucester Cathedral, Harford

Lloyd and Lee Williams (known as the " Father of the Three Choirs ") ; some of the musical critics, and the house-party. The room was full; and all the lights were turned out except for some device arranged by Frank Schuster for lighting the piano and the violin-stand.

Sir Edward took his seat at the piano, and after a tense whisper to me—" You are not going to leave me all alone in the *tuttis*, are you ? "—we began. My qualms vanished: I became so thrilled by the atmosphere created, by the evident appreciation of the listeners and the magnetic force that flowed from Sir Edward, that I threw my whole heart and soul into the performance, realising that the soloist is, after all, but the servant of the composer, and that he must strive to render, not merely the notes and the brilliance of the passage-work, but the inmost thoughts and the most subtle shades of meaning expressed in the music. That evening is a never-to-be-forgotten memory to me ; and I always, as I think of it, feel deeply grateful to him for giving me such an artistic experience.

The orchestration of the concerto was already finished (on August 5th). Fritz Kreisler arrived towards the end of the Gloucester Festival week and at once began to study the concerto for the first public performance, which took place at Queen's Hall in London on November 10th of that year. Such was the energy of Elgar at this period that, as soon as the concerto was finished, he was writing another *Pomp and Circumstance* March and correcting proofs of the concerto and other things, besides lending a helping hand and giving the benefit of his advice to Ivor Atkins (organist of Worcester Cathedral and conductor of the Worcester Festival), who was engaged upon a new edition of Bach's *St. Matthew* Passion. Elgar was also laying plans and getting ideas on paper for the Second Symphony.

When the concert (November 10th) was over, nearly all his time and energy went to the new symphony, which grew apace, so that it was finished on February 28th, 1911. After this he went on a tour in the United States of America and Canada (I received a postcard inscribed "Deleerious deevil," to let me know that he had started), but found time to write his Coronation Music, which he conducted in Westminster Abbey on June 22nd. The Coronation March was played also at St. Paul's Cathedral on June 29th.

The Worcester Festival took place in September, at which was performed the new edition of Bach's *St. Matthew* Passion, bearing the inscription "Edited by Edward Elgar and Ivor Atkins."

To understand even superficially the complex personality of Elgar, it is necessary to know how quickly he could change from grave to gay, from the utmost seriousness and solemnity to a light and humorous mood. After conducting a moving performance of *The Dream of Gerontius* or *The Apostles* in the cathedral, he would return to the house and change all

32

his clothes, and with them his mood. Then he would begin to chuckle over the amusing things that had happened to him in previous Festivals either here or elsewhere.

At one of the Festivals, Lady Elgar took a house which was in term time a boarding-school. Having numerous bedrooms, it suited her purpose admirably; for there was to be a large house-party. Upon the arrival of the guests, and when they were being shown to their various rooms, it was discovered that none of these was furnished with a bell or other means of communication with the domestic staff. Sir Edward at once saw his chance and took it. He set off to the local toyshop and bought up everything that would produce an individual sound. Then he drew up a scheme for the various bedrooms, as follows:

No. 1. Rattle   No. 4. Toy drum
No. 2. Tin trumpet   No. 5. Penny whistle
No. 3. Squeaker   etc.

and hung up the list in the kitchen. He told me it was worth while waking up early in the morning to hear Mrs. Worthington appeal plaintively on the penny whistle from her door, or Frankie Schuster blow a fanfare on the tin trumpet from his, or three or four of them together set up a din which only his trained ear could disentangle.

It was about this time that I first noticed how a sentence, however frivolous, or perhaps only a word, would run in his head almost *ad nauseam*, just as a fragment of a tune will do. I have known others, including myself, have this obsession; and I mention it because it had some influence on his music. Once I heard someone make a remark on some trashy music. I haven't an idea what it was, or who wrote it; but the person I was with said it was " jossy." The next time I met Sir Edward I mentioned this. He was so delighted with the expression that he kept on repeating it. " Jossy ! " he would say and then clap his hands on his knees and roar with laughter. When we were playing the concerto, and I waxed enthusiastic about any passage, he would say, " I don't mind *what* you think about it, as long as you don't think it ' jossy.' "

Another word which haunted him was one he had picked up from a story about the Edinburgh Lunatic Asylum. I think he was conscious of the fact that he could tell a story remarkably well. He never minded repeating a good one any number of times, nor did his own enjoyment of it ever seem to wane : certainly he took infinite pleasure in relating this particular Scotch story—at great length sometimes, if he were in the mood. Briefly it was this :

When the interior of the Edinburgh Lunatic Asylum was being repainted, the painter was instructed to make no reply should any of the inmates address him during his work. Unfortunately, the first person to address him was an Inspector of Asylums, who was visiting the institution officially.

34

" How many coats of paint are you going to put on that door ? " he demanded. No reply. Inspector: " Do you hear me, fellow ? I am asking you a question." No reply. Inspector: "Are you deaf or only stupid ? Are you aware that I am the inspector and that I am addressing you ? " The painter could stand it no longer. Looking round at his persecutor with terror in his eyes, he shouted, " Gang awa', ye deleerious deil," and fled.

This word " deleerious " was the joy of the whole story; I have seen it written in many places on Elgar's MSS. If any passage worked up to a terrific climax he would write over it " deleerious."

Another favourite was " Moglio." I saw this written over a passage in *In the South* and asked what it meant. " Oh," he said, " it is only the name of a village where Carice and I were in Italy." Carice is Sir Edward's daughter; and I learnt from her afterwards that he kept repeating this ridiculous name until at last he actually put it into his music.

Full score, p. 17. Fig. 10. Second bar:

Clarinet in B♭ (sounding a whole tone lower). Answered by first violins:

and again on pp. 18, 19, and 20.

If a section in any music under discussion was not consistently kept up to the level of the earlier part, his criticism was, " It seems to have gone off the boil." He picked this up, I think, in the farmhouses where he and Carice would ask for tea on their country rambles, and where the kettle was not always " on the boil." At all events, it served him on all occasions. " Oh, he's gone off the boil," would mean that someone had ceased to write articles for a certain paper, or that he had given up cycling or golf, or that his enthusiasm for the theatre or the opera had waned. Applied to the garden it would mean that the rose-trees had ceased blooming.

In a letter I received dated August 9th, 1910, Sir Edward wrote, " I have no more proofs yet—the word ' boil ' has been removed from the printers' vocabulary." This followed another, dated July 13th, 1910 : " I have been expecting more proofs, but none have come—the printing seems to have gone off the boil."

When Elgar was seriously critical, as of his own music, nothing was too good for him. When his sense of humour was roused, nothing was too absurd. The supreme valuator suddenly became quite childlike.

One of the constant visitors at Plas Gwyn was, naturally enough, Dr. G. R. Sinclair (G. R. S. of the Enigma Variations), organist of Hereford Cathedral. He was a great Elgar enthusiast and loved to call and chat with him. He was also a cyclist ; and if he could

PLATE II : THE ELGAR BOYS WITH THEIR FRIENDS

EDWARD HAS THE BASSOON AND FRANK THE OBOE

persuade Sir Edward to go cycling with him he was in the seventh heaven. After one of their expeditions Elgar said to me, " You know, Sinclair is a funny person: he is a dear and I am very fond of him; but his ideas of companionship and mine differ materially. Yesterday he came up here and said, ' What a great day ! I am going to persuade you to leave work for a little while, and come out cycling with me. We will go up over the hills and round through this place and that, and so on; and it won't be too tiring for you.' The words were hardly out of his mouth when he pedalled off at full speed, and I followed as fast as I could, just keeping him in view for some miles until we came to a steep hill. At the top he got off his machine and waited for me, just drinking in the view. I was pretty nearly done, and was looking forward to a rest. But the moment I came up to him he said, ' Isn't the view from here magnificent ? But we mustn't stop too long to admire it: we must push on.' And up and off he went, coasting away down the other side of the hill like an avalanche. And he did that every time. At the top of every hill he would dismount and wait until I came up panting; but the moment I was within speaking distance he would expatiate upon the beauty of the spot until I was close up. Then he would warn me again that we mustn't stop: we must push on—and so ride away furiously. This went on until I saw him dismount outside my own gate and wait for me to catch up with him for the last time, thank heaven !

' Grand ride we have had together,' he shouted as soon as I was within earshot. ' I *have* enjoyed being with you '—and off he went to his own home. As a matter of fact, I had scarcely been near him, had never ridden a yard by his side; but *he* enjoyed it. Sinclair *is* a funny fellow."

One of the amusements at Hereford at this time was throwing the boomerang. When we were tired of our musical jobs we used to go to one of his beloved spots, a meadow down by the Wye River, and practise with the boomerang, watching its peculiar flight and constantly striving to acquire the necessary skill to bring it back to our feet at the end of it. Once, Edward was almost too successful. The wretched thing circled all over the meadow, then, suddenly altering its course for no apparent reason, it made a bee-line for us. We ran like hares and barely escaped with our lives, for it was about eighteen inches in length and fairly heavy. It whizzed round in the air at a terrific speed and looked quite capable of taking off both our heads if it had caught us under the chin.

Another diversion at Plas Gwyn was The Ark. This was the name given to an outhouse which had been converted into a laboratory—the inside furnished with shelves and a bench and innumerable bottles, retorts, Bunsen-burners, test-tubes and all the paraphernalia of an analytical chemist. Here Elgar would retire and ease the burden of his destiny as a composer by pretending to be a chemist.

One day he made a phosphoric concoction which, when dry, would "go off" by spontaneous combustion. The amusement was to smear it on a piece of blotting paper and then wait breathlessly for the catastrophe. One day he made too much paste; and, when his music called him and he wanted to go back to the house, he clapped the whole of it into a gallipot, covered it up, and dumped it into the water-butt, thinking it would be safe there.

Just as he was getting on famously, writing in horn and trumpet parts, and mapping out wood-wind, a sudden and unexpected crash, as of all the percussion in all the orchestras on earth, shook the room, followed by the "rushing mighty sound" he had already anticipated in *The Kingdom*. The water-butt had blown up: the hoops were rent: the staves flew in all directions; and the liberated water went down the drive in a solid wall.

Silence reigned for a few seconds. Then all the dogs in Herefordshire gave tongue; and all the doors and windows opened. After a moment's thought, Edward lit his pipe and strolled down to the gate, *andante tranquillo*, as if nothing had happened and the ruined water-butt and the demolished flower-beds were prehistoric features of the landscape. A neighbour, peeping out of his gate, called out, " Did you hear that noise, sir : it sounded like an explosion ? " "Yes," said Sir Edward, "I heard it : where was it ? " The neighbour shook his head; and the incident was closed.

At night, when the members of the family had gone to bed, he would stride up and down the room telling of his difficulties in the past; how slow people were to recognise anything outstanding in his music, and how they could not understand that a young man who played in a band, and went about teaching the fiddle in Malvern, Worcester, and neighbourhood, could possibly be a composer. They could see that he was always writing music of sorts, but regarded this as a kind of hobby to be treated with indulgence. The Serenade for Strings was played at a concert, and then neglected for years. It was only when he at last obtained some measure of fame with the Enigma Variations that people began to look up the serenade and other works of that period and to assume that they must be great because they were the works of a Great Man.

He told me how once, when he was staying at Norwood in South London, and had been writing most of the day, he thought he would like to go out for a stroll; so, after changing into an old suit and putting on a cap, he set out in the direction of London. He walked on and on, thinking of what he had been writing, and turning over new ideas in his mind, until he found himself in the Borough High Street, close to London Bridge, and near a second-hand bookshop. As usual, the books were displayed in rows outside the shop as well as within, and some interesting title or old specimens of binding attracted him so that he stopped to examine them more closely. He turned them over one after the other until he could scarcely see, as it was growing dark; then finally, picking up a book he had a fancy for, he went to the door of the shop and enquired the price. "One shilling," said the bookseller. Sir Edward's hand went into his pocket, and found—nothing! When he changed into the old suit, he forgot to change the contents of the pockets. He had not a penny with him.

Feeling very perturbed and still grasping the book in the gathering darkness, he explained to the book-seller—whose expression seemed rather forbidding by this time—that he was very sorry, but, as a matter of fact, he hadn't the necessary shilling, nor even any money at all for that matter. "I thought as much," said the bookseller. "I have had my eye on you for some time, young man: you drop that book and bunk."

Now the comedy of this incident lies in the fact that Elgar was a great man, and the bookseller did not know it. Yet Elgar was modestly unconscious of this or he would never have told the story.

Another incident that Elgar loved to relate in those days occurred when he was staying in the country and wanted to orchestrate. Alas! he had no scoring-paper with him, nor any paper large enough for the neces-sary lines. However, the nearest town was but a few miles away; so he walked over to it. There he found a general sort of musical emporium—the sort of place one sees in country towns, where saxophones, piano-accordions, mouth-organs, banjos, zithers, and ocarinas prevail to the entire exclusion of the classical orchestra, except perhaps a couple of bright red or sickly yellow violins, and a tutor with a picture of Paganini squirming diabolically at a spellbound audience.

In walked Sir Edward. A young man at the counter regarded him expectantly. Edward, thinking he would not be likely to know what scoring-paper was, tentatively asked, " Have you any music-paper ? " The young man, without deigning to reply, produced some ordinary twelve-stave paper. " Oh, yes," said Sir Edward; " but I mean paper with twenty or twenty-four staves on a page." " Oh ! you mean scoring-paper," said the young man witheringly. After a search somewhere at the back, he emerged triumphantly with a brown-paper parcel, which contained exactly what was wanted.

A certain number of pages having been counted out, the young man, now taking an encouraging interest in his customer, remarked, as he was tying up the parcel, " Going to try your hand at a bit of scoring, eh ? " " Well," said Elgar, with his most modest air, " I thought I might try and do something of the sort." "Ah," said the young man knowingly, " you'll find it a jolly sight harder than you think— you take my word for it." Elgar, to whom his music came orchestrally ready-made, and who never could understand how a musician could be in any doubt as to how to score a passage, retired wondering whether he ought not to have urged the unfortunate young man to take medical advice.

Elgar was intensely fond of the country. Like William Morris, he was in love with the earth. He seemed to me to know every inch of Worcestershire (his own county), Herefordshire, the Malverns, Gloucestershire, and the Severn and Wye Rivers. He never tired of talking of them, exploring and re-exploring them if only to see again all the things he knew to be there; and his great joy was to have a kindred spirit with him to share in these pleasures, and to see his own joy reflected in the face of another. Side by side with this went his great love for humanity, especially the village folk, and those in the humbler walks of life. Position or station were nothing to him in his dealings with his fellow creatures; but the things they said and did were for him of inexhaustible and abiding interest. He gave me the impression that he could remember without the slightest effort everything that anyone had said or done within his experience, with the date and every detail complete. This is of course impossible; but, if only I could remember a tenth of what I gleaned from listening to his conversation on our many jaunts in a two-seater car through the highways and byways of Worcestershire, I should be an extraordinarily well-informed man. He would point out to me every village, every house, every peculiarity: the landscape, the old main line to Worcester running three miles from the city owing to the prejudices of the city fathers, who proved beyond the shadow of a doubt that all vegetation would die for at least half a mile on either side of the line, poisoned by engine-smoke. The existing loop line to the city was a repentant afterthought.

We visited all his boyhood's haunts, the tiny cottage at Broadheath where he was born, which looks exactly the same to-day as in his earliest recollection. Many is the time we have taken the dogs up there for a run; and, while they were romping, I have had all the landmarks, including the very trees that were there when he was a boy, pointed out to me.

He never minded referring to his early days or to his position among the County people, by whom his father was always treated as a gentleman and a friend. His father had to use his talents in all musical directions, whether it was getting up a little band—which, when the Elgar children were growing up, could almost be done without going outside the family (see Plate II)—or arranging the music for the local reception, ball, or any function requiring music: writing out the band parts, or composing the music if nothing suitable could be found. In this way Edward became responsible for numerous sets of quadrilles, lancers, marches, and anything that was wanted to help his father, to whom everyone came

44

for anything musical. Piano-tuning was the outdoor department of the music-shop; and Elgar senior condescended to nothing less for his conveyance than a thoroughbred, until Edward was old enough to accompany him, when a pony and trap or a dogcart had to be substituted. When a piano had to be tuned at Croome Court or at Madresfield the boy Edward was taken for what was practically a delightful day's outing. While the piano was being attended to he could roam about in the grounds until he was taken into the house and refreshed. No detail or happening of those far-off times escaped him; he could tell me as we ambled about the lanes and passed these great houses, and many others too, the names of all the people who lived in them long ago, and relate to me the sayings of the members of the household, or the yarns spun for his benefit by the groom, or the old ostler who watered his father's horse.

We once passed a mark made with a piece of straw up in the top of a hedge. His eyes glistened as it reminded him that one of these old fellows told him when he was a boy that when he saw that mark it meant that someone carting hay had "accidentally" lost a truss. The mark meant that the missing truss was to be found two or three hundred yards farther along, well concealed behind the greenery. When we passed the house where he had given his first violin-lessons, he could remember the name of the pupil, the year and even the month, and how important he felt as he dressed himself carefully to act as the professor for the first time.

Also I heard about the time he spent before that in a lawyer's office, and the things he learnt there. He retained an unexpected knowledge of legal affairs, and had all the legal vocabulary at his tongue's end. He had been given responsible work, too; and it was delightful to hear the note of pride in his voice when he told me how the firm had remarked to his father that Edward was a " bright lad."

The lawyer's office was not for him, however; and soon the call of music became irresistible and he had to follow. He managed to scrape enough funds together to take him up to London, where he studied the violin with Pollitzer, of whom he always spoke with the greatest admiration. His ambition then was to become a famous violinist; and for this he worked unceasingly. At his first lesson, after he had played and been criticised, he was told to get a certain book of studies. At his next lesson, when he produced this book, Pollitzer said to him, "Now, which one of these have you prepared for your lesson to-day?" "All of them," said the young student, having been at them night and day, in fact, until he had mastered them.

While he was in London he took the opportunity of going to every possible concert; and he always spoke almost reverentially of those which August Manns conducted at the Crystal Palace. I think it was the attendance at those concerts—when he heard that

PLATE III : ELGAR AND HIS FATHER

orchestra play the great classics and saw the romantic figure of the young conductor with his plume of raven hair (to me known only as a white-haired and most dignified old Prussian gentleman), interpreting the works of Beethoven and Schubert, Mendelssohn and Schumann, with occasional ventures into Liszt and even Wagner—that fired his ambition and turned the scales on the side of serious composition. He realised that he must be first and foremost a creative musician. He was bubbling over with thoughts and ideas that clamoured for expression.

When his violin-lessons had to end he went back to Worcester to take up a position as violin-teacher and orchestral leader, going all over the country to the various concerts where he or his friend Charles Hayward (whose name was always being quoted when he related these incidents) had to lead the orchestra.

Judged by our modern standards, these concerts given by the local choral societies were evidently scratch affairs; but they were important enough in their own consciousness, being taken up as first-rate social functions and very well attended. If there were two horns instead of four, or any other discrepancy, or if a serious mishap occurred in the *ensemble*, not many people in the audience knew any better, or enjoyed the music any the less; these things really added to the enjoyment of the evening, besides providing a topic for heated discussion for many days after the event.

47

At a rehearsal for one of these concerts, the conductor was nervous and a little on edge; so, to commence the proceedings, he timidly raised his baton aloft, gazing hopefully at the leader of the orchestra. He, as soon as he saw the conductor raise his arms, at once held his violin in position with the bow raised for attack. This tense situation, accompanied by an impressive "Bayreuth hush," lasted for what seemed an eternity. Then, as nothing else occurred, the conductor lowered his arms and resumed his original position. Looking more nervous than ever and not a little puzzled, he finally decided that this oratorio must begin somehow, so up went his arms again and up went the violins of the orchestra with bows held at the ready. Still nothing happened, the conductor and the leader staring at one another in anguished expectation. The hush was broken at last by the former, who, in a reproachful aside that could be heard all over the room, said, " Well, Mr. Elgar, if you do not begin, *I* shall." " Oh, is that what you are waiting for ? " said Mr. Elgar; and with that he and Charles Hayward put their heads down and let into it with a will, leaving the conductor hopelessly behind.

After the rehearsal had been proceeding for some time, one of the prominent members of the society came up and, cupping his two hands, shouted into Mr. Elgar's ear, " Cut it short, Ted lad: there's a red-hot leg of mutton just gone into Mr. Ogle's." The conductor overheard, and turned the tables on his leader by winning the race to Mr. Ogle's easily.

In December 1911, Sir Edward had to be so frequently in London that he left Plas Gwyn, and, after spending Christmas at the house of Lord Charles Beresford at Brunswick Terrace, Brighton, took up his residence at Severn House in Hampstead. This was a beautiful house, very high up and containing a wonderful studio on the first floor. At the far end a door led into another, smaller room which was his library and his den; and here he wrote *The Music Makers, Carillon, The Spirit of England, For the Fallen, The Fringes of the Fleet, The Crown of India*, etc. (these works are not quoted in exact order, but as they occur to my mind). He was very busy, I remember, at the time that he was composing *The Crown of India*, and he sent me an S O S one day to come and help with some of the orchestration. Such an invitation was always more than welcome; but we had not been at work very long when, amid intense excitement, a billiard-table arrived, and was duly installed in another good-sized room leading out of the main studio. After that *The Crown of India* faded out. A day or two later the telephone bell rang—I answered—Sir Edward's voice speaking—when could I come and play billiards? Now, I don't know whether other people had the same experience as I had with that billiard-table; but I never once succeeded in getting Sir Edward to *finish* a game. We would get as far as 30 or 40, or perhaps even 50; but

DH

he always switched off to the study of diatoms—he had added a microscope to his *ripieno* instruments—or went to the piano and played, or fetched out a full score to show me in dreadful secrecy how Wagner had evidently made a close study of the Haydn quartets before composing *Die Meistersinger*. I have seen three beautiful microscopes at once on that billiard-table, with slides, condensers, and everything complete, strewn all over it. Whether the extra microscopes were for his guests, like teacups, I could never quite make out; but I suspected that he enjoyed having companions to share his appreciation of the marvels revealed.

As he said, " It is a grand place for a microscope, just under the lights and at just the right height to gaze into the eye-piece."

Personally I much preferred this diversion to the ordinary game of billiards: a game at which I have no skill. But that did not matter; for, as far as I could gather from our interrupted attempts, Sir Edward hadn't very much more himself, although, as in everything else he set himself to do, he was dead serious about it, and would never attempt the most obvious shot until he had thought out exactly where the balls were likely to be, not only for the next shot, but for the one after that. It was too brainy for me—for either of us, I imagine, as I look back on the scene—at any rate, after these exhausting calculations, the obvious shot was missed more often than not; so the rest of the plan did not materialise; and it was my turn to take the cue and make either a *faux pas* or a fluke, after which the calculations were resumed with Einstein-like intensity.

Many people attributed his divagations to a strain of perversity in his character, forgetting that, to a professional musician, music is work and play is anything except music.

He came to me one day and said that a dear old friend of his, Mr. Edward Speyer, who lived at Shenley, wanted him to go there for a week-end and take me with him. Mr. Speyer was nearly, if not quite, ninety years of age at this time, but he was very lively, which made it difficult to realise that he had arrived at such an advanced age. He had been a personal friend of Brahms, Goldmark, and many other famous musicians of his time; and music was his one subject. Knowing this, I took my violin, expecting that there would be music on the Sunday. This expectation was considerably reinforced when upon arrival we were told by Mrs. Speyer that Madame Suggia was coming later on in the evening.

Unfortunately for our host's plans, Sir Edward had just learnt a new game at the billiard-table, a kind of pool with coloured balls. I don't think it was the ordinary game known as snooker; and I am not quite sure that Elgar didn't make up the rules himself, with probably the assistance of Hugh Blair, from whom I fancy he learnt the game, as Blair was

51

frequently in and out of Severn House at this period; for Edward's extraordinary fertility in variations was by no means confined to music. At any rate, as soon as tea was over we had to go at once to the billiard-table and learn the new game. This went on until it was time to dress for dinner. Then Suggia arrived. During dinner the new game was explained to her, with the result that, after coffee, Suggia, Mrs. Speyer, and myself had to begin a fresh game with him. In vain poor Mr. Speyer produced some sheets of music to discuss with Sir Edward. They were glanced at hurriedly and put down again because it was his turn to play. The game went on until bedtime.

The same thing happened next day. We played a new variation of the game for a while in the morning; then Sir Edward and I went out for a ramble. After lunch he had his afternoon rest; and then at last Mr. Speyer got in some interesting first-hand anecdotes about Brahms, Strauss, and others, which took us on until dinner. Mr. Speyer tried hard to get Edward into a musical mood. He even brought out some of his part-songs which he had there, hoping to interest him; but no: nothing could interest him for long except that new game, which we all played again until bedtime. Next morning, full of sincere thanks to our host and hostess for a most enjoyable week-end, and taking our farewell also of Madame Suggia, we left Elstree without having played a single note. Mr. Speyer might as well have entertained Lord Lonsdale.

Soon after the performance of the Second Symphony, Sir Edward became very busy with the music for *The Crown of India*; and, amongst a quantity of smaller works, *The Music Makers* (a congenial setting of O'Shaughnessy's finest poem) and the orchestral study, *Falstaff* (regarded by many musicians as his greatest orchestral work), were all composed at Severn House during these years before the War.

It is true that, in the summer of 1913, Sir Edward took a house at Penmaenmawr, where he spent much time revising and correcting proofs of *Falstaff* before it was produced at Leeds Festival in the October which followed; but the actual composition of all these works took place at Severn House, when he was not playing with the microscope or poring over heraldry and the ancient history of anywhere or anything (but principally Worcestershire).

In June 1914, Mr. Henry Embleton took the Leeds Philharmonic Choir, which was conducted by Dr. Coward in those days, to Canterbury Cathedral, and gave a grand and unforgettable performance of *The Apostles*. The London Symphony Orchestra was engaged and Sir Edward conducted. The effect of this work, played and sung as it was in that cathedral, was profound. It must have been a huge encouragement to the patron of this Yorkshire choir, Henry Embleton, whose hobby it was to stimulate Dr. Coward to train it to the highest possible level and then take it about, at no matter what financial loss, to sing in London,

53

Canterbury, the provincial musical centres in Great Britain, and eventually to Paris.

In August the War began, and Sir Edward became a special constable in the Hampstead Division on August 17th. He was very excited about it, and donned armlet, belt, and hat; he also had a truncheon, which he handled rather gingerly, I thought. I certainly could not imagine his using it in any circumstances, and I trembled as I thought of him going out to perambulate the streets at any hour of the day or night and in any weather, firmly grasping his truncheon and looking about for the German spies and dynamitards with whom our imagination peopled every dark corner, characters whom I prayed he might never meet.

My relief was very great when I heard that he had resigned in the following February; but it was not long before he joined the Hampstead Volunteer Reserve. While he was a "special" he wrote the music to Emil Cammaerts' poem, *Carillon*, set as a recitation with music. This was first performed at the Queen's Hall on December 7th, 1914, and was most moving, as it described very vividly the sufferings of the Belgian nation in the first days of the War, when their country was overrun.

On December 10th, Sir Edward gave a concert at Severn House in aid of the Belgian refugees, and shortly afterwards went on tour all over England and Scotland with Percy Harrison of Birmingham, an impresario who organised these provincial tours each year. The London Symphony Orchestra, with the Belgian pianist, Arthur de Greef, and Constance Collier, who recited *Carillon* in French, formed the concert-party.

When we were in Edinburgh one Sunday, Sir Edward and I took a taxi-cab and drove out to Queensferry on the shores of the Firth of Forth. We could see across to Rosyth, where several cruisers which had been engaged at the Dogger Bank were being overhauled and having their wounds attended to. We were very thrilled about the submarine nets which we were told stretched right across under the Forth Bridge—and then we drove back and thought how awful it all was, and how much we hoped that it would all be over quickly.

After the tour, Sir Edward was soon busy again, and at the earnest wish of Mlynarsky he composed *Polonia*; and afterwards set Binyon's *For the Fallen*, in which he was able to resume once more his own noble, natural style. I, being enlisted under the Derby Scheme and doing war-work, was luckily not sent away, so was able, though there was not much time for music in those terror-ridden days, to get together a few string players and take them up to Severn House to try over the string parts for Binyon's poem. This we did also with *Drapeau Belge* and *The Spirit of England*, Sir Edward filling in the wind parts on the piano. Then followed the setting of Kipling's *The Fringes of the Fleet.* This was performed at the Coliseum and ran for some time, Sir Edward himself conducting at every London performance (it was being performed also in the provinces), a task which he really enjoyed while it lasted.

Soon he began to long for the country; and, as it was not advisable to go too far away, Lady Elgar found the ideal spot at Fittleworth in Sussex. The house, Brinkwells, was a country cottage with a lovely garden, surrounded by acres and acres of woods and chestnut plantations. There was a separate building in the garden, evidently built as an artist's studio, as it had a very large window on one side, looking across a stretch of grass which sloped away downhill and seemed to me to be the only clearing in these thick woods for miles.

Sir Edward was charmed with this place; and he had not been installed there very long before I had a letter inviting me to come as soon as possible. When I arrived, Mr. Aylwyn, a neighbouring farmer, met me at the station with a pony and trap, it being rather a long way to Brinkwells and difficult to find unless one was acquainted with the district; also I had a bag and a fiddle-case. We jogged along through some wonderfully wooded country, along a road which twisted and turned continually, until at last we came to about half a mile of straight road rising up a fairly steep hill, with chestnut plantations on either side. At the top of the hill, looming on the sky-line, was what at first sight I

PLATE IV : THE MUSIC ROOM AT SEVERN HOUSE WITH LIBRARY BEYOND

took to be a statue; but as we drew nearer I saw it was a tall woodman leaning a little forward upon an axe with a very long handle. The picture was perfect and the pose magnificent. It was Sir Edward himself, who had come to the top of the hill to meet me, and placed himself there leaning on his axe and fitting in exactly with the surroundings. He did these things without knowing it, by pure instinct.

We had to send Mr. Aylwin on to the house with the trap containing my belongings; for Sir Edward could not wait another moment to introduce me to the very heart of these woods, and to tell me all about the woodcraft which he had been learning from the woodmen who earned their livelihood here. Chemistry, physics, billiards, and music were abandoned and forgotten: nothing remained but an ardent woodman-cooper.

We soon came to a primitive kind of shack, round which were piled numbers of newly cut chestnut-poles. In it were contrivances for stripping and splitting these poles, making hoops for barrels, and doing all sorts of things in that craft of which I could make nothing. Sir Edward had picked it all up, and was now bubbling over with excitement as he explained it to me.

Then, as we walked up to the house, he told me which part of the wood went with it, and how he had the right to cut any wood there except forest-trees, which, I gathered from him, included oaks, beeches, and elms. I was glad to hear it; for he had another axe ready for me, and apparently expected me to handle it there and then as expertly as my violin-bow. He set me at once to cut down some chestnut-poles. Happily, before I had time to cut myself down, Lady Elgar wanted a tub for some domestic purpose or other; and, as there was a big barrel up at the house doing nothing, he produced a long two-handled saw with which we sawed the barrel in halves quite successfully and presented Lady Elgar with two tubs. A sudden relapse into experimental chemistry was precipitated by a plague of wasps in the garden, the greengage-tree being the attraction. Cyanide of potassium was clearly indicated; so he obtained some from the local chemist, and arranged that we were to go out about an hour before sunset, to intercept the wasps on their return to their nest.

I was not surprised when, after tea, Lady Elgar took me on one side and said, " I am so glad you have come: it is lovely for him to have someone to play with."

Then into the wood with the axes, Sir Edward explaining how all low brushwood must be cleared away so that nothing should impede or divert the single stroke of the axe—the correct way to fell these chestnuts. We cut a few in this manner by way of practice, and hauled them up to the tool-shed to trim them into stakes for our fence.

After dinner the wasps' nest had to be dealt with, so

Sir Edward, with the deadly bottle and some cotton wool in his pocket, took me out to show me the nest—a hole in the bank in a very dry spot. There were one or two wasps entering or coming out, so Sir Edward put some cyanide on to a wad of cotton wool and pushed it a little way into the hole with his walking-stick. Then we both lit our pipes and sat down on the opposite bank to watch.

Very soon a wasp arrived, tried to enter, staggered back, and dropped dead.

Hundreds soon littered the ground in front of the entrance, so that the new-comers had to scrape their bodies out of the way to get to the hole, adding their own bodies to the heap. Sometimes one would get only half a whiff of the poison: he would then dart about in the air, flying in a wild and erratic manner until he dropped dead in the road, or returned to the hole for another sniff, which put an end to his career. We sat there until it was nearly dark; but, as no more wasps seemed to be returning, we decided to go back to the house and dig out the nest next morning. Sir Edward said that the grubs would be splendid bait for fishing.

We retired to bed soon after we reached the house; but I woke up about half-past four in the morning to find Sir Edward standing by my bedside fully dressed, with a pair of Wellington boots which he wanted me to put on. He had on a similar pair of boots himself. When we went out, the extraordinary coldness of the

dew-drenched grass convinced me of their necessity
He was perturbed because he had been seized with
an uneasy feeling about those wasps which lay in
heaps on the road. It suddenly occurred to him that
children going early to school would see them and
might be led up to the hole, where they would find
the wool with the deadly cyanide on it. He could sleep
no more, so came to fetch me.

While I was dressing, he fetched a spade and
fork ready; and off we went to the spot as soon as
possible. We were relieved to find everything exactly
as we had left it the night before. The hole was quite
covered with dead wasps; but there were no dead
children, so we knew nobody had meddled with the
cyanide.

Sir Edward said it would be quite safe to dig the
nest out now, arguing that most of the wasps had been
away from home when we started operations, and any
that were in would have come to the entrance to get
out and been slain inside. Accordingly, we proceeded
to dig, not very successfully at first, as the wasps had
used an old mole-run for a tunnel, so that the nest
was not as near the hole as we anticipated.

Suddenly I plunged the spade into the very middle
of the nest, or so it seemed. Turning up a huge clod
of earth, I uncovered a most intricate and paper-like
structure beneath. We only saw it for a fraction of
a second, however; for the din that arose, as of a
million wasps all buzzing at once, sent us flying. I

had just enough presence of mind to replace the clod of earth before we bunked. After removing and burning the wool with cyanide on it, we went back to the house to fetch Mark. We explained the situation to him; and he, rising to it without the least discomposure, procured two large pails of boiling water and accompanied us back to the scene. I lifted the clod of earth once more and Mark dashed the pails of nearly boiling water one after the other into the nest. We dug it out later and extracted the grubs—which were all in little cells like honeycomb—for our fishing.

Mark was a character. He went with the house, like the tool-shed or the chestnut wood. I don't think he had ever been more than five or six miles from Fittleworth in his life. He looked after Sir Edward's comforts and helped about the house and garden. He was a man of few words, very unimpressionable. He made no comment whatever about the wasp episode: he only looked at us both with what I should describe as a pained expression, if so impassive a face could be said to have any expression. Mark was a character after Sir Edward's own heart. His monosyllabic replies were quoted again and again.

On one occasion, Sir Edward, finding that there was no music-stand in the studio, went down to the tool-shed and knocked up a very creditable one. Standing back and surveying his handiwork with his head a little on one side, he became aware that Mark had entered and was standing looking at it, too.

" You see I have made a music-stand, Mark," said Sir Edward. " Mr. Reed is coming, and will want something to put his music on. I am afraid it is rather rough; but then, you see, I am not very handy with tools."

" No," said Mark dully, and walked away.

One of Mark's jobs was to empty the waste-paper basket. When the daily torrent of circulars, requests for autographs, and begging letters overflowed, Sir Edward would be moved to apologise.

" I suppose they must send it all to *somebody*," was all Mark ever said.

When Sir Edward was sketching the 'Cello Concerto at Brinkwells, he asked Felix Salmond to come down and try over what he had written. Mark went to the gate to help Felix in with his luggage, which included the monstrous black coffin of the 'cello. Then Mark gazed for a moment at Felix, and silently withdrew.

Later, Sir Edward said to him, " Mark, that gentleman who came to-day with the big case is a very famous musician, a great 'cellist, a very important person, you know."

" Well, I suppose," said Mark, to console him, " it takes some of all sorts to make up a world."

It was at the studio at Brinkwells that the three Chamber Works were written.

At my first visit the Violin Sonata was well advanced. All the first movement was written, half the second—he finished this, actually, while I was there—and the opening section of the Finale. We used to play up to the blank page and then he would say, " And then what ? "—and we would go out to explore the wood or to fish in the River Arun.

His fishing was really one of his recreative poses; for, though he cut a most effective figure on the banks, we never caught anything but the smallest and most innocent of fishes, which we took carefully off our hooks and put back in the river for the fun of watching them swim gleefully away.

Soon the Sonata was finished, and the Quartet and Quintet well under way. Sir Edward wrote out most of the quintet—all the second movement—for violin and piano, so that we could play it more comfortably, as it was rather difficult for me to pick out parts from his MS. looking over his shoulder.

A favourite short walk from the house up through the woods brought one clean out of the everyday world to a region prosaically called Flexham Park, which might have been the Wolf's Glen in *Der Freischütz*. The strangeness of the place was created by a group of dead trees which, apparently struck by lightning, had very gnarled and twisted branches stretching out in an eerie manner as if beckoning one to come nearer. To walk up there in the evening when it was just getting dark was to get "the creeps."

I am sure that this spot had a profound influence on the three Chamber Works: witness the mystical and fantastic theme of the second movement of the sonata.

The rather oriental and fatalistic themes in the quintet, and the air of sadness in the quartet, like the wind sighing in those dead trees—I can see it all whenever I play any of these works, or hear them played. Elgar was such a nature-lover and had such an impressionable mind that he could not fail to be influenced by such surroundings. There was so powerful a fascination for him there that he was always strolling up to look at the scene again.

Sir Edward and Lady Elgar returned to London in October; and we played the finished sonata many times, Sir Edward playing the piano part himself. Later, when I played it in public—at the Æolian Hall—I shared the honour with Sir Landon Ronald.

After the signing of the Armistice, Sir Edward returned to Brinkwells until the end of the year, working at the details of the quartet and quintet, which we frequently played with violin and piano in the studio. We also played over something he had sketched while he was on one of his London visits and which he said was to be a 'cello concerto. The sketch is interesting because it is covered with his comments as usual, but they are inscribed with a typewriter instead of in his own handwriting. This was a new toy, and had to be used. The instrument did not lend itself to variations except in its black and red ribbon. The original jumps from one colour to the other in the most erratic manner.

On January 1st, 1919, he was again back in London;

and I was presently summoned to attend with the other members of my quartet to try over the new works, which were now practically finished, the string parts being all copied and ready.

This I arranged for January 7th; and on my arrival a little in advance of the others I found four stands set out in that beautiful room, a large card inscribed " Reed's Jazz " being placed on the one nearest the door. The few guests who were allowed to come included the Bernard Shaws, whom I met for the first time.

In Cobbett's *Cyclopædia of Chamber Music* I have written a chapter analysing and describing these works, and I cannot improve on a short paragraph therefrom concerning the slow movement of the quintet : " It opens with a sublime melody entrusted to the viola. It abounds in finely shaped and polished phrases; and, with its warmth of expression and inspired moments, it appears to have grown like some work of nature, without the help of human hands." Only a hopeless pedant would attempt a technical analysis of such a piece of music, which expresses all the higher emotions of which humanity is capable. It expresses them so truly, and goes so much further into the hidden meaning of things than any mere words, that it seems to be a message from another world.

During that year, my colleagues and I played these works frequently, sometimes with Sir Edward at the piano in the sonata and quintet, also later on with William Murdoch.

One bright sunny day we all went down to The Hut at Bray-on-Thames, and played them to a select circle in that delightful studio by the river; Mr. and Mrs. Ernest Newman were there on this occasion, among other notable people. We went there again in September, and then gave several performances with Albert Sammons, Felix Salmond, William Murdoch, and myself. In June, Sir Edward went down again to Brinkwells and worked hard at the 'Cello Concerto, which was soon finished, scored and ready for performance. Felix Salmond played the solo part at Queen's Hall on October 27th that year at one of the concerts given by the London Symphony Orchestra, Sir Edward himself conducting.

After this, Sir Edward did not write very much of importance, only a few small pieces, part-songs, etc. But he was never idle for a moment. He went to Brussels and Amsterdam to conduct his works; when he came back he busied himself about some literary work and continued his investigations with the microscopes.

In the beginning of the New Year, 1920, Lady Elgar seemed to be ailing. She who had always been so full of vitality and energy was now often listless. She would creep up close to the fire and look so fragile that I began to feel anxious about her. She would brighten up for a little while; but every time I saw her she

PLATE V : BRINKWELLS (WHERE ALL THE CHAMBER MUSIC WAS WRITTEN)

seemed to be getting smaller—she was never of any great stature—and I am sure she must have been losing weight.

The greatest tragedy of Sir Edward's life came upon him on April 7th, when Lady Elgar died. He was quite prostrated. I do not know what he would have done without his daughter, Carice. Upon her he leaned with all his weight; and she bravely sustained him and helped him through that terrible time.

The funeral was fixed for April 10th at St. Wulstan's Church, Little Malvern. Frank Schuster and Carice begged me to bring my colleagues to play the slow movement from the String Quartet. Lady Elgar loved it; and they thought it would comfort Sir Edward a little.

I hurriedly arranged this: and Sammons, Tertis, Salmond and I went to Malvern and played in the little gallery at the west end of the church. It was very sad to see Sir Edward there with bowed head, leaning on Carice's arm.

As I left the gallery and prepared to follow the coffin to the graveside, a hand was placed convulsively upon my arm and a voice said, " Tell him I had to come. I dare not go to the graveside as I am not well, and my doctor absolutely forbids me to stand bareheaded in the open air; but I felt I must come: do tell him for me," and with that the speaker buried his face in his hands and walked away in tears. It was Sir Charles Stanford.

It was fortunate, perhaps, that at this period Sir Edward had many engagements which could not be sacrificed to his private grief. He had to conduct *The Apostles* in Newcastle in May. After that he went on a short tour in South Wales with the London Symphony Orchestra. In June he received a new decoration, *L'Ordre de la Couronne*, from the Belgian Ambassador. This brought him within a couple of months of the revival of the Three Choirs Festival at Worcester after the terrible war years. He spent them at Brinkwells, The Hut, and other places.

At Worcester he lodged in a small house in the college precincts, and lived very quietly. When we went for walks along the banks of the Severn he became very reminiscent, telling me all about his early married life, and when Carice was born, and everything that had happened year by year up to the time of Lady Elgar's death. In the evenings, so that he should not feel dull, I always went to his room, when I came out of the cathedral, to play cribbage with him: a game which he always enjoyed and over which he became quite excited. I imagine he had played it a good deal in his youth, for he was so quick to see all the possibilities, and loved marking on the cribbage-board. He had taught me the rules when I first went to Fittleworth.

After the Festival he was very quiet, and seemed quite disinclined to write any music. I tried once or twice to lead him on by asking him about the third part of the Trilogy (the two parts from *The Apostles* and *The Kingdom* being completed). He had a cupboard full of sketch-work for it; and once or twice I succeeded in getting him to play me some of it, in the hope that I should set him on fire once more and get him to complete the trilogy. But I could not stay with him all the time; and, the moment I went away, it all went back into the cupboard and nothing was done.

The following year he grew by degrees more cheerful; and as the spring drew on he became quite his old self. I was delighted when he told me he was going down to Brinkwells again; for I had hopes that it would have the same effect on him as before, and that the sight of those woods and all the things he loved would set him off again in a new direction. He was very happy there, and enjoyed playing works he had already written. Hopefully I took my violin there. But never was there anything new for me to play.

One day during the summer of that year (1921), Dr. Percy Hull (organist of Hereford Cathedral and conductor of that year's Festival of the Three Choirs at Hereford) came to Brinkwells to discuss rehearsal arrangements and other details for the forthcoming Festival. We all spent a delightful day wandering about in the woods, playing some of the new Chamber Music, and generally enjoying life until it was time for Dr. Hull to start back to London. He said he would rather walk to the station than ride; and Sir Edward was in his element telling him how he could go down through the woods, turn here, turn there, keep on over the bridge, etc., etc. The directions were repeated so often in such meticulous detail that it was clear to me that Percy's brain was overtaxed. However, he took an affectionate farewell and set off confidently down the open space by the studio, disappearing into the woods in the right direction.

When he had gone, I had my violin out, and after we had been playing for the best part of an hour, happening to look out of that large studio window, I suddenly saw a black-coated figure emerge from the wood, carrying a little bag and striding along at a great rate as he made for another opening in the wood on the opposite side. He looked strangely familiar; and I called Sir Edward's attention to the apparition. He gave one glance out of the window, and rushed to the door with a " Hallo ! " which caused the black-coated figure to stop short in his stride and turn round. The look of astonishment on Percy Hull's face when he realised he had been walking hard in those woods for the best part of an hour, and then found himself back at Brinkwells, was indescribable.

After the summer, Sir Edward, having disposed of Severn House, took a flat in St. James's Place, close to St. James's Street and the many clubs to which he belonged. I think he had an idea that he had perhaps kept himself too much aloof, especially avoiding the younger generation of composers and conductors; so he asked me to come and help him give a luncheon party at the United Services Club, St. James's Street.

He invited John Ireland, Richard Strauss, Bernard Shaw, Eugène Goossens, Arthur Bliss, Rutland Boughton, Adrian Boult, Arnold Bax, Norman O'Neill, and many others. They nearly all came, champagne flowed, and Sir Edward made a most excellent speech, to which there was a very happy response, and we had a very jolly party. Shaw questioned the composers as to whether they had a sense of absolute pitch, which most of them disclaimed. I forget whether he took the opportunity to ventilate his favourite contention that Strauss derived, not from the German school, but from Donizetti. Afterwards, when we two went back to the flat at St. James's Place and discussed it all, I felt that it had done him a lot of good, taken him out of himself and cheered him considerably; so that my hopes of getting him to begin composing again were renewed.

I was still more elated when he decided to go back and live in the country, and took Napleton Grange, a house at Kempsey, just outside Worcester on the Tewkesbury road. He kept on his London flat in St. James's Place for some years, as he needed it for his frequent trips to Town. At Napleton, Marco, the black and white spaniel, and Mina, the little Cairn, appeared. These two famous dogs, both of whom—but especially Marco—appeared in numberless photographs with him for many years, lived with him for the rest of his life: they were his constant and adored companions. They were both miserable whenever he went away, and their joy on his return was something to witness; they rushed about in a wild state of excitement, Marco with one of his master's gloves in his mouth, which he would not give up, and Mina getting under his feet and doing her best to trip him up. How happy he was there with the garden and the beautiful surrounding countryside, and with Kempsey Common close at hand, where he could walk with the dogs without fear that they would come to any harm.

Mary Clifford, his devoted secretary and housekeeper, was here also, taking care of him and looking after his dogs whenever he had to be away from home.

Mary Clifford had already been doing secretarial work at Severn House for some time. After the death of Lady Elgar and after the marriage of Sir Edward's daughter, Miss Clifford took up her position permanently in the Elgar household, where she devoted herself whole-heartedly to him and his affairs until his last days; when she shared with Carice the daily and nightly vigil by his bedside right up to the end of his life.

I went down there continually with my violin. He suddenly had a fancy to play some of the old violin-music; so he went into Worcester and borrowed some Spohr concertos, and lesser-known sonatas like the Rubinstein in G major, a suite for violin and piano by

Ries, and much other music of that sort which he thoroughly enjoyed playing. He never tired of playing the piano accompaniments to these pieces. I think they brought pleasant memories to him; for he had played the fiddle part to most of them in his violinistic days. They nearly always set him " reminiscing " and recalling the " stylish " way he and Charles Hayward used to " let into it."

I never met Charles Hayward; but his name was always cropping up, when Sir Edward would stand up to his full height and play an imaginary violin with the wildest abandon, singing some phrase out of one of the old pieces at the top of his voice, moving his imaginary bow about at incredible speed with a white-hot enthusiasm, and telling me that this was how he and Charles Hayward electrified the natives on their old rounds. I always thought that he was acting the old pictures of Paganini on these occasions.

He seemed so tall when he drew himself up, and had such a purposeful expression on his face. The *pièce de résistance* was when he imitated Wilhelmji, whom he had heard play the *Air Hongrois* by Ernst. From his account of this affair Wilhelmji must have had a colossal tone; and his attack on the opening tenth on the G string must have been hair-raising. It excited

73

Elgar to such an extent that he never forgot it; and when he showed how it was done I felt thankful he was content to perform upon an imaginary violin and not on mine; for the movement he made would have cut any ordinary violin in half.

I tried very hard in these days to induce him to work at Part III of the Trilogy; but he did not show any enthusiasm, and always said, "Oh, no one wants any more of that nowadays"; but he would nevertheless sit down at the piano and play portions of it; and the old light would come into his eyes as he worked himself up and began grunting away to himself, his hands meanwhile flying about the piano. He never could sustain the mood, however, and so no more of what he evidently had in his mind materialised on paper. What a loss ! When one comes to the last bar of *The Kingdom*, and realises that Part III can never be written now, one could weep.

He used to tell me about it. It was to depict the Last Judgment, with the Shofar *motif* from *The Apostles* for the last trumpet. He apparently had it all planned, but could not face the drudgery of putting it on paper. The mainspring was broken somehow. I say somehow, because even now it is not certain whether he was disabled by the beginnings of his physical breakdown or by a loss of faith in any real necessity for any more oratorio. He never talked about his religion; but he was obviously more sceptical generally as a widower than he had been during Lady

74

Elgar's lifetime, and, as we shall see, turned finally to opera and secular music only.

About this time, while at Napleton, Henry Embleton decided to take the Leeds Choir to Paris. Sir Edward was to conduct *The Dream of Gerontius*, the Second Symphony, and *Sea Pictures*. Dr. Coward of Sheffield was to conduct some Handel: *Israel in Egypt* choruses, and some from *Messiah*. The London Symphony Orchestra and a quartet of soloists were included in the trip. There were two concerts in Paris and one at the Casino at Dieppe, the latter luckily taking place on the way back, as the crossing from Newhaven to Dieppe was none too good, and I for one was very much overcome. Sir Edward insisted on giving me his cabin, so that I could lie down; and he mothered me the whole way over and did all he could for me, he himself being quite unaffected by the choppy sea.

The hotel where Sir Edward and I stayed in Paris was near the tomb of the Unknown Warrior; and, when I came down the first morning, I saw an enormous wreath lying on the floor in the hall with the French and English colours intertwined and a card from the Leeds Choir. It was waiting for a deputation from the choir to take it and lay it on the tomb of the Unknown.

There was quite a stir amongst the other visitors about this; and an American lady who was sitting at the next table to mine asked me if I could tell her

75

about it. This I did; and I also told her that the Leeds
Choir was giving a grand concert that afternoon with
the London Symphony Orchestra, and that Sir
Edward Elgar was going to conduct his Second
Symphony.

The concert in the afternoon was very well attended,
the audience very enthusiastic, and Sir Edward had
an ovation at the end of his symphony. He was very
hot and much worked up. We took a taxi and went
back to our hotel. We had taken only a few steps over
the threshold when my American friend of the morning rushed up to Elgar and, in a gushing torrent of
American adoration, told him she had been to the
concert, and how " too thrilled " she had been at
seeing him conduct, and how " too cute " the Scherzo
was, etc., etc., all in one breath. Before she had time
to draw another, he stared at her coldly and walked
off upstairs to his room. The poor lady turned to me,
consternation written on her face, and said, "What
is the matter? Have I said something wrong? " I
replied, "No; you said nothing wrong: everything
you said was perfectly charming, the only thing was
you said it at the wrong time." Then I explained to
her how wrought up he was, why he had to hurry
and change his things after conducting and getting
very hot, and that he was overcome for the minute
by her sudden onslaught, not knowing in the least
who she was. I promised that when he had changed,
I would bring him down and introduce her to him.

PLATE VI : BRINKWELLS — EDWARD SELECTING SUITABLE WOOD TO MAKE A WALKING-STICK

So, though I had really no case, I went up to Sir Edward's room and expostulated. "I did not know she was a friend of yours or I would have spoken to her," he said. "I never saw her in my life until this morning," I said; "but I made her buy tickets; and I felt very sorry when she looked so crestfallen after you had walked off in that way. Her feelings were horribly hurt." He said nothing. I tried again. "Won't you come and speak to her just for a moment with me, just to let her know that you were not really offended?" No reply. With all the pathos I could summon up, I demanded, "Is she to go back to America with a completely wrong impression of you —you of all people!—who I know would never hurt anyone's feelings wilfully?" That moved him to reply. "Where is she now?" he said. "We will go and speak to her." I formally introduced her to him; he spoke to her in his most charming manner without referring to his previous behaviour; and she, let us hope, felt consoled, and perhaps honoured by the experience.

I have told the story here as very likely he may have behaved like this on other occasions, and been completely misunderstood in consequence. He was naturally shy, and wanted to get away from most people, especially strangers, when he was busy; and I do not think he often stopped to consider what effect his methods of accomplishing this had upon the intruder, his one idea being to escape as quickly as possible. He was the soul of courtesy and had the kindest heart in the world. He was incapable of intentionally hurting any innocent person's feelings in cold blood, even if he disliked them; but in self-defence he *would* do these things and leave a wrong impression upon the minds of those who did not know him.

On returning to Kempsey he settled down again to the life of a country gentleman, reading a great deal, studying, and pursuing various hobbies, and running up and down to London, Manchester, Bournemouth, Hanley, or wherever he had to go to conduct his works.

At this time he began to take the gramophone very seriously. He was like a child with a new toy when his friend Fred Gaisberg, artistic director of H.M.V., sent him the very latest machine with a truly marvellous reproduction. Mr. Gaisberg always kept him up to date in this respect; every improvement or new invention that came on the market was at once installed, the old machine being removed and the new one substituted; so that all his favourite records had to be played over and over again on the new machine.

I had to be in attendance to note each subtle difference; and woe betide me if my mind wandered and I let anything pass without comment, or without registering at least some fraction of his excitement and enthusiasm. One day he had a new contrivance

78

which was a great thrill. It enabled him to sit in
an arm-chair away from the machine, and, by
pressing a button on the arm of the chair, increase
the volume of sound to a deafening *fff* or diminish
to *ppp*.

Berlioz's *Sinfonie Fantastique*, especially the March
to the Scaffold and the Witch's Sabbath, also the
descending trombone passage at the beginning of the
Fire Music at the end of Wagner's *Die Walküre*, came
in for some drastic experimental treatment with this
new device.

All very exciting and stimulating. How his face lit
up and expressed every note in the emotional scale !
And how he would watch my face to see if I could
follow him in these transports ! It is an abiding joy
to have been with him so much and to have shared
his varying moods so closely.

"*Now*," I used to think when I had got him well
worked up in some of these musical transports " now
is my opportunity to get him back to work, to his
real life's work"; and I would lead him to discuss
the details of his Second Symphony or the orchestration of *The Apostles* or *The Kingdom*. Then I would
suggest that the sketch-work and scraps belonging to
Part III be fetched out of the cupboard and played
over. My violin would come out; and I would play
over his shoulder anything suitable, until I thought
I had roused him sufficiently for him to continue
after I had gone away. But nothing came of it: he

79

was through with oratorio; and I had to try a new tack.

So I tried to get him to start thinking of a third symphony. This was the right line; for I believe he often dreamed of it; yet never in all the years at Kempsey and Tiddington Court or Battenhall Manor did he write anything down or produce anything that he could show me or that we could play together. When others asked when a third symphony would be forthcoming he explained that he could not afford to compose symphonies, as they cost many months of work and brought him in practically nothing. And, as this was unfortunately a hard fact, it closed the discussion.

He wrote from time to time part-songs or smaller pieces, also the music for *King Arthur*, a production which ran for a time at the Old Vic.; but this was more or less incidental music and the sort of thing which he could produce without much thought and certainly without effort.

It is not, therefore, music of any abiding value; nor is it like his large-scale work, on which he had expended his whole heart and soul. But it is symptomatic of a fancy for the theatre which, as I shall tell presently, might have borne fruit in an opera if his talent had really been of that kind.

Meanwhile, though he would not work seriously at his music, he was the most delightful and lovable companion. He was always busy about some hobby or another, and he made me feel that his enjoyment of them was at its height when he had me with him to share it.

He loved his house—Napleton Grange—at Kempsey; and he was very sad when, at the end of the lease, he found he could neither renew it nor buy the place. So he started looking for another house.

This he found outside his beloved Worcestershire, at Stratford-on-Avon. It was called Tiddington House.

In it he settled down and seemed very happy. The River Avon flowed along the bottom of the garden; so the fishing-rods were brought out and set up all ready for the correct fishing mood to come upon him: he also bought a very smart rowing-boat.

I had to rush to Stratford to inspect all this, and explore the river, which is certainly very beautiful in either direction from Tiddington.

Bonfires were another diversion. The garden was large, and there was a lot of litter and garden refuse to be disposed of. When a huge heap had accumulated, a postcard would arrive advising me that all was ready and waiting for me to arrive for the grand lighting-up.

Then there was the food. Someone had sent him a case of fizzy Spanish wine, like champagne. It was a great success. We had to have a bottle up after bonfiring or boating; then we would get into the car and go over to Leamington, where " the best sausages in

England " were on sale in a certain shop he had discovered and thenceforth visited in person once a week.

On returning from one of these expeditions we had to pass some pleasure gardens where a band was performing. We slowed down to catch a strain of what they were playing. It was the *Meistersinger* overture; so we stopped the car and went in to listen. Fancy our feelings when the overture suddenly changed into the Jewel Song from Gounod's *Faust* ! This too became bedevilled, and melted into Grieg's Anitra's dance from *Peer Gynt*, which in its turn melted into " variety," presently solidified into the *Tannhäuser* march, and wound up with *Chant sans Paroles* by Tschaikowsky.

Elgar was furious, spluttering, as we fled back to the car, " Don't they want to hear any piece played through properly; or can no one nowadays listen to more than a few bars of anything without getting bored ? "

He was really angry about it, and said it would not matter so much if they made their potpourris from the jazz tunes and the lighter music, but to drag the classics into such company and make them ridiculous was to corrupt the taste of the young and degrade the world's musical heritage.

Unfortunately this sort of thing accentuated his disinclination to compose; so I hastened to change the subject.

82

He loved all the old music that he had loved as a boy. The tide of fashion in this respect passed him by as it did me; and we were alike in that we both still loved music which was quite taboo in precious circles. Elgar's boyish pleasure in Suppé did not in the least interfere with his relish for Stravinsky; and the fun he got out of *L'Oiseau de Feu* or *Petrouschka* never put Mendelssohn, Gounod, Grieg, and Schumann out of court.

He loved Schumann, and would discuss his symphonies at great length. The music entranced him; but he felt the weakness of the orchestration. He often surmised how certain other composers with a gift for orchestration would have scored this or that passage —what Wagner would have done with it, or Berlioz, or Richard Strauss; and I knew by the light in his eyes that he had a complete picture of it in his head, and knew very well what he himself would have done with it. But he felt strongly that the personality of the composer should not be overshadowed by anyone else attempting to " improve " upon the original. He would point out weak spots in the orchestration in Brahms's symphonies—the concluding chord of F major at the end of the first movement of the Third Symphony was one of his favourite examples; but he would not have altered the lay-out of this chord for worlds, nor would he have countenanced anyone else's " tinkering with it," as he would have expressed it.

He was always amused too by the appearance of the triangle at the end of Brahms's Variations on a Theme of Haydn, known as *St. Anthony*. He used to say that when old Brahms wanted to get a bit festive, towards the end of the Finale, the only thing he could think of was to introduce a triangle. Whenever he heard this, or looked in the score and saw it, it always brought a broad smile to his face.

Similarly he was immensely pleased when he heard those passages which he had noticed himself when he had first taken part as an orchestral player in such works as *Elijah* or *Messiah*. Year after year at the Three Choirs Festivals, his head would appear round a pillar in the cathedral to catch my eye when the altos and tenors enter, with their A♭ and F respectively, in the concluding bars of "All we like sheep" (*adagio*). He revelled in the sweeping passage for the violins in "Thou shalt break them," and was disgusted when one year we played from Prout's edition and found the bowing to which he had been accustomed altered so that this broad sweep of the phrase was in his opinion ruined. As to the entries of the sixths (referred to above) in the *adagio* at the end of "All we like sheep," so simple on paper, so colossal in effect, it made him, as he described it, "cry like a cow." At any moment he would rub his hands gleefully and look up to heaven at the thought of old Handel's genius.

Oddly enough, the scruples he felt about meddling

84

with the orchestration of Brahms and Schumann did not prevent him from rescoring some of Handel's overtures and revelling in the exquisite but audacious variations which Mozart imposed on the instrumentation of *Messiah*, to say nothing of his arrangements of certain Bach fugues for full modern orchestra. He defended the Mozart embroideries on the ground that they were just what Handel must have improvised himself when he was filling in at the organ. And he quite reasonably contended that to tamper with what Schumann had done with a modern orchestra which was ready to his hand was quite a different case from showing what Handel or Bach could have done had they possessed such an instrument.

The overture to *Elijah* he would never miss. He pointed out to me that Mendelssohn was the first composer to touch up the entries of the successive voices in the Fugue: the horns coming in on the last beat of the second bar of the exposition; then the clarinets and bassoons at the sixth bar, later the oboe: none of them taking any part in the statement of the Fugue subject, but holding sustained notes against the moving parts of the strings, adding colour and great sonority to the whole texture.

Many other things in *Elijah* pleased him intensely, and he loved pointing out Mendelssohn's use of the trombone, and his cleverness in directing the first violins, in " Cast thy burden," to hold on the top note of the chord long after the other notes had ceased, " to keep the vocal quartet up to pitch."

When Mr. Gaisberg sent him the records of the Fantastic Symphony of Berlioz, he played the March to the Scaffold again and again to enjoy the devilish commentary on the situation by the three bassoons, and the use of the side drum (solo) and the blazing chord at the end. I suggested that this meant the cheers of the frenzied multitude after the knife had fallen.

He did not mind confessing to a great liking for the Coronation March by Meyerbeer. His eyes used to shine with excitement when we discussed this and hummed the strong rhythmic tune: the strength of that triplet on the first beat of the bar gripped him.

A mutual friend of ours, Her Highness Margaret, Ranee of Sarawak, an excellent pianist and a very discerning musician, told me that she went to see him once and he insisted on playing over the whole of Gounod's *Faust* with her as a piano duet. She said it was great fun and they both thoroughly enjoyed it.

Elgar's tastes in music were all-embracing: he liked nearly all music that had tune, rhythm, or colour. He loved some of Bach's music, but by no means all; and he had no great affection for the Elizabethan composers. Byrd he pronounced insipid except for a few works. He liked Purcell, but would not join in the furore about Tudor music that arose amongst a certain

86

PLATE VII: NAPLETON GRANGE. ELGAR AT WORK

set of young composers who apparently could see no good in any music between the Elizabethan madrigals and the *Sacre du Printemps* of Stravinsky.

He would not rave about folk-tunes. I don't think he ever made use of one in his works. He held that the business of a composer is to compose, not to copy. Certainly the second subject in the Introduction and Allegro for Strings has a slight folkish flavour; but that was because he was sitting out on the Malvern Hills one day when some Welsh people were having some sort of gathering a little way off; and, as they always do when they get together, they burst into song. Their music came to him on the wind as he sat there alone. Their tunes and phrases were nothing to him; but he seized on the effect with which, whatever they were singing, the interval of a falling minor third seemed to predominate; so he wrote the subject,

etc., which, though entirely his own tune, shows how susceptibly he could extract the honey from wild flowers. I suspect that the tune of the *canto populare* from *In the South* may have come to him on the wind in Italy in the same manner.

No music was written at Tiddington House so far as I can remember; but I was sorry when he told me one day that his time at Stratford was coming to an end and that he was looking out for a new home.

It was sad having to leave the river, and the boat and all the things he had grown to love. He never found the ideal house and garden to take its place.

He took Battenhall Manor at Worcester—the house of a friend of his, Mrs. Sybil Buckle—for a while, to look about for a place to settle down again. And then, very characteristically, he went off on a liner to South America and sailed up the Amazon about a thousand miles or so. He came back very full of his experiences; but the Amazon impressed him less than the fact that in South America, in places with quite a small population, the opera house was the handsomest and most important building in the town. The contrast with our own want of vision, especially with regard to the drama, and opera in particular, was not lost on him. One magnificent opera house—I forget which—quite excited him. It was after this trip that he began to talk to me of opera and the possibility of his composing one.

I jumped at this promise of renewed activity and urged him to tell me more of what he had in mind; but, as usual when anything very important was brewing, he became reticent and rather mysterious, saying, "Ah! well, we shall see," and the like.

Meanwhile, a house called Marl Bank, on Rainbow Hill in the city of Worcester, was chosen for his future home. He moved in there and at once settled down with Marco and the other dogs. The excitement of a new environment, new gardens, new fruit-trees, and a multitude of new interests, at first left no time for music. I tried again to lead him back to the missing third part of the great trilogy, *Apostles*, *Kingdom*, and *Last Judgment*; but it was useless: he seemed to have quite made up his mind that no one would wish to hear any more of that, in spite of my repeated assurances to the contrary.

His mind was evidently veering to another quarter. He was quite ready to discuss a new orchestral work, and even definitely a piano concerto and a new symphony. At all events, I could see that there was something working at the back of his mind; and I grew hopeful.

Marl Bank is not very far from Malvern; and G. B. S. frequently came over to see him when he was staying there for the annual Drama Festival; so that at this time I was always hearing about what he had said or done, etc.

He had, in fact, asked Shaw to write an opera libretto for him. Shaw replied that his plays set themselves to a verbal music of their own which would make a very queer sort of counterpoint with Elgar's music. He suggested that Sir Edward should take his play *Androcles and the Lion* and just try setting a page of it to music. " You will find," said Shaw, " that you cannot make an opera of it, just as you could not make an opera of Shakespeare's *Henry IV*. But you may make another *Falstaff* out of it. That is really your line."

Evidently Shaw was not his man, right as he may

have been; for Sir Edward was stage-struck and wanted to play at opera-making. He therefore called in another Malvern friend, Sir Barry Jackson, who indulged the new fancy in the most sympathetic and helpful way. It was not long before I came upon fragments of music-paper on the piano, in the blotter, all over the house, in fact, with an unaccountable B. J. in the corner.

I have a letter from Sir Barry describing how it began. Here it is:

"When Sir Edward told me that it had long been a wish of his to compose an opera, my first impulse was to inquire as to his libretto; and it was no surprise to hear that his inclination ran in the direction of that full-blooded dramatist Ben Jonson. What did surprise me was that, instead of taking one of the better-known plays, he had set his heart upon *The Devil is an Ass*, a work which always appeared to me to be quite moribund. After renewing acquaintance with this comedy, I wrote saying I felt nothing could be done with it. A fortnight later I was overwhelmed by the sensation that I might be standing between the world and a great musical work, and earnestly applied myself to the not-easy task of disentangling the imbroglio of the play in question. Diving through the voluminous spate of words and incidents, I found at the bottom what seemed to be a splendid story for an opera, which proved that

Sir Edward was right from the first. I delivered a rough MS. founded on the plot and text of the play, with interpolations of the poems for the more lyrical moments, and with this he appeared to be delighted. He had given me his copy, which was liberally covered with jottings and suggestions, obviously a labour of love carried on over a long period. The story was fined down to the uttermost dramatic limits in my version; but Sir Edward was determined that the work should be on a grandiose scale; for he added incidents and complications without end, always declaring that, if ever he composed an opera, it was going to be a grand opera.

"Amongst his music were numberless sheets of MS. with a large B. J. in the corner. It would have been just like him to honour me by asking my assistance, rather than that of someone better equipped, simply because of the similarity of the initials."

From conversations I have had with Sir Barry since, also from remarks Elgar himself dropped on the subject, Elgar was very headstrong and not a little difficult when he had conceived a situation on the stage in a certain way (perhaps not very practical from the theatrical standpoint); and when Barry Jackson, with his vast stage experience, came along and put his finger unerringly on a weak spot, summer lightning would ensue. Elgar would alter an idea *here* in deference to Barry's judgment, perhaps; but he would fight for an idea *there* until he had convinced Barry that it *was* practicable.

Soon the music grew until there was a pile of MS. on his desk. As has been said, every scrap of the projected opera had B. J. on it in large letters, a fact for which I was more than thankful when the task fell to me later of searching through all his scraps of MSS. for anything relating to the unfinished Third Symphony. I always thought that B. J. stood for Barry Jackson, and it was a very long time before I suddenly discovered that it stood for Ben Jonson.

Elgar became more and more enthusiastic about this; and we began playing a lot of it on my violin and his piano. There was a Spanish dance, a country dance, a bolero, and a saraband. Also numerous vocal portions of which I played the voice part whilst he accompanied vigorously and excitably at the piano. We could have earned our living with it at a provincial café, *al fresco*. Then we talked it all over. It was to be Grand Opera on the biggest scale: a tremendous work, in fact. He would explain with a wealth of detail everything that was to happen on the stage at the particular bar we were trying over. He would even draw a plan of the stage, showing all the "properties" and exactly where the characters were to stand; but if I am ever asked what it was all about I shall have to confess that I have not the faintest idea, and never had. I only know that Sir Barry told me that

Elgar had seized upon the name of one of the characters in the play for a title, and the Opera was to have
been called *The Spanish Lady*. How tragic that this
opera, with his Pianoforte Concerto and Third
Symphony, can never be finished.

When the British Broadcasting Corporation suddenly intervened miraculously with a commission for
a third symphony, and Sir John Reith, as *deus ex
machina*, made a handsome provision for the spade-
work of composition as well as the main payment for
the performing-right, everything else had to be put
aside until the symphony was complete. That was the
end of the Opera. It was, alas ! the end of all work for
Elgar.

Meanwhile, however, his life flowed on evenly and
happily at Marl Bank. He went up to Town frequently
to conduct performances to be recorded for the gramophone, a job which he thoroughly enjoyed; and each
year, at the Three Choirs Festival at Worcester,
Hereford, and Gloucester, he added lustre to these
meetings by the incomparable performances of his
works under his own baton in the cathedrals.

His gift for repartee and his ready wit never forsook
him: indeed, he became, if possible, sharper and
quicker in this respect as he grew older. I remember
very well an instance of his quick rejoinder at one
of the Gloucester Festivals.

A memorial tablet in memory of the late Sir Hubert
Parry was to be unveiled in the cathedral; and for this

event Sir Herbert Brewer had gathered together as many notable musicians as possible. Before proceeding into the cathedral he invited them all informally to meet one another on his lawn. The local photographer, hearing of this, came upon the scene with a purposeful glint in his eye and soon had these notable people suitably grouped for his purpose. They were Lord Gladstone, Sir Henry Hadow, Sir Charles Stanford, Sir Hugh Allen, Sir Granville Bantock, Dr. Lloyd, Dr. Hull, and Sir Edward himself. They were all in morning dress, as it was just before the morning meeting in the cathedral.

Elgar, as was his habit, had his smart morning-coat buttoned up with military tightness; and easy-going Sir Hugh Allen, who stood next him in the group, said:

" Now then, Elgar, don't have your coat all buttoned up like that."

" Ah ! " said Elgar; " I always keep *everything* buttoned up when I am in *this* company."

On another occasion he was taking his little Scottie, Meg, out for a walk on a lead, not realising what a lump of energy a little dog like this can be. After being tugged and tripped about for an hour or two he was accosted by a humanitarian female who relieved her misplaced sympathy by exclaiming, " Oh, what a shame having a lively little dog like that on a lead ! " " You are mistaken, madam," said Elgar; " it is I who am on the lead."

After the sad and sudden death of Sir Herbert Brewer in the spring of 1928, Mr. Herbert W. Sumsion, who was then in Philadelphia, was appointed to succeed him as organist of Gloucester Cathedral, and recalled to take up his duties there, also to conduct the Festival, which happened to be at Gloucester that year. This was rather an ordeal for a young man to face; and everybody was very glad when he emerged successfully at the end of the Festival week. Sir Edward's congratulation was, " Well, John "—he is always called John—" what at the beginning of the week was assumption is now a certainty."

He " dated " in being the last of the Victorian punsters; for he loved words—the jingle of words— twisting them about so as to alter their meaning, much as he did with his musical themes and ideas.

He said to me on the spur of the moment, after a performance of a new piece of mine called *The Lincoln Imp*: " Well, Billy, I hope it won't make your income limp."

Lady Elgar's names were Caroline Alice; so his daughter is named Carice. The house he lived in for a long time in Malvern—where I think he wrote the Enigma Variations—was called Craeg Lea, an anagram compounded of C. A. E. and ELGAR. Needless to add, he was an adept at crossword puzzles, and would lavish priceless time on the solution of the abstruse ones.

He was like a child in many respects; and although

when I suggested any frivolous amusement or did anything boyish he would rebuke me with " Oh, Billy, when, if ever, will you grow up ? " he was much the same himself. One of the Gloucester Festivals occurred when the " Beaver " craze was in vogue. He made me play this game with him, the rule being that, if we met a man with a beard, the one who cried " Beaver ! " first scored one, except when it was a *red* beard, when he scored three. We actually set out through the streets of Gloucester, our scores mounting, and Sir Edward's excitement culminating when he spotted two red beards approaching, and got in his " Beaver ! " each time before I had even seen them. My triumph came later, in a narrow street where most of the shops sell curios and antiques of all sorts. Outside one of them, propped up for all to see, was an illustrated volume open at a page depicting Assurbanipal, the bearded monarch of ancient Assyria.

As soon as I spotted it, I fairly yelled " Beaver ! " When Sir Edward recovered from the shock, I added : " Let's write ' Beaver ' on a card and put it in front of the picture."

Whether anyone saw the revered composer of *Gerontius*, and his orchestral leader, behaving in this fashion, I cannot say. I hope not.

When we returned through that street a little later on—walking as unconcernedly as possible on the opposite side of the road—we found that not only had the inscription been removed, but the volume itself had gone. Sir Edward claimed that we had done the bookseller a good turn and sold his old book for him.

How delighted he was one day when my little car petered out and I couldn't find why it wouldn't go ! We had only just filled up with petrol at a garage a little way back. At last, in desperation, I walked back to the garage to fetch a mechanic. On our return we found Sir Edward sitting serenely in the car as if it was all the same to him whether it moved or not. The mechanic said simply, " You 'aven't turned on the petrol," and turned it on. Sir Edward roared. I paid.

Sometimes our motorings took us to spots that had played a part in his earlier life. " Let's go over to Birchwood," he would say, and then direct me down all the narrow lanes and byways he knew so intimately, telling me about it as we drove. He wondered if they had ever finished staining the floor of the room in which he had scored *Gerontius*. While he was there he got so tired of seeing the bare boards between the mats or rugs in the room which was his den, that he persuaded Lady Elgar to get some walnut-staining. Then, very characteristically, he left his proper work and bent all his energies on staining the floor. He stained it so thoroughly that when he had used up the liquid there was a patch still unstained. There was nothing for it but to cover it with a mat until some more staining could be obtained. And, as this never happened, the floor is piebald to this day, or was when we visited it a few days before Christmas, 1932.

He showed me the window in which he sat working at the full score of *Gerontius*, and the lane where Lady Elgar used to go to meet the postman each evening, with the completed pages which had to go daily to Novellos' in London to be engraved.

It seemed to me such an ordinary cottage until I was overcome and not a little awed by the knowledge of what had come out of it !

I could not help contrasting Elgar with those composers who need some special environment—stained-glass windows, the interior of some great church, or at least a mascot on the table—before they can compose.

I think Elgar could have written any of his works at the top of the Alps or the bottom of a coal-mine. His music came from within, and the outer surroundings did not exist for him when he got down to the donkey-work, writing the music first in short and then in full score. He worked at great speed, oblivious of anything but the sounds he was carrying in his head.

At the same time, he liked to revisit in after years the scene of his labours. I expect it brought back some of the original thrill of putting on paper all the magic with which we are now so familiar.

When I stood there and thought of those trombone chords which accompany the priest's " Proficiscere

PLATE VIII: MARL BANK
(ELGAR AND MINA IN THE PORCH)

anima Christiana " in Part I, or the passage " Like the deep and solemn sound of many waters," I marvelled that these vast things had come out of that small cottage.

Edward came away in a very quiet and subdued mood. I would not talk either, very much, as I knew where his mind had gone, and felt it almost like sacrilege to say anything.

Then would come one of his breezy transitions. He would rouse himself quite suddenly and say, " Drive back over the bridge, Billy; and we will call at that place by the theatre and see if we can get some oysters. You would like some oysters this evening, wouldn't you ? And I don't know what *you* feel like, but I could drink a pint of beer."

Another reminiscent drive was to Longford Marshes, a place at the back of beyond somewhere between Tewkesbury and Ledbury. I am rather hazy about the exact spot, though we often drove in that direction: he loved it because it was off the main roads and very unfrequented.

Here he used to sit and dream. A great deal of *The Apostles* took shape in his mind there. He told me, despite what I have just said about being able to compose anywhere, he had to go there more than once to think out those climaxes in the Ascension; for they had to be so built up each time that they never reached such a pitch of intensity as at the last and greatest climax, or he would have felt that the architecture of this movement was imperfect. It was indeed a problem.

Suddenly he would switch off this solemn subject to tell me how he varied the Ascension by falling off his bicycle hereabouts. This led him to tell me about a device he had fitted to lock the front wheel so that the machine would stay leaning against a tree or wall in safety, the wheel being rigid instead of wobbling about.

He had been a little troubled with toothache, and one day, while writing in his music-room at home, the tooth was worrying him all the time he was trying to work out a complicated problem of orchestration. Putting down his pen in desperation, he decided that he would proceed at once to the nearest dentist and have the wretched tooth out. With his usual precipitation he rushed out, snatched the bicycle from the wall, and mounted it. A violent header over the handle-bars reminded him that he had forgotten the so-called safety-catch that locked the front wheel.

When he picked himself up his toothache had ceased entirely, and did not return; so he always after this believed that an unexpected shock was an infallible cure for toothache. I told him I preferred toothache, as at least you *knew* what you were in for.

Another day he said, "Put a bottle of that Spanish wine in the car, Billy: we will go up and see old one of his old Malvern friends immortalised in one Troyte." Troyte was Troyte Griffiths, the architect, of the most virile of the Enigma Variations.

When we arrived Troyte was out, and we could not make anyone hear: so Sir Edward said, " Never mind: put the bottle behind the door. Troyte will know where it came from: it will do him good."

On our way back from Troyte's he paid a visit to another old friend, Miss Norbury—W. N. of the Variations—who was ill in bed, and had been so for some time. He was always ready to visit any old friends of whom he was fond, especially if they were ill; and it always visibly did them good to see him. He was so gentle and sympathetic that it was wonderful to be with him and to see him so closely in all his varying moods.

Some of his reactions from music into the more commonplace human excitements were more unexpected. For instance, one of his refuges from the tyranny of his genius was the Turf. Part of his enjoyment of this, I feel sure, was derived from the queer names of the horses and the jargon of the racecourse. But he made a study of it as he did of everything he took up, and mastered the whole betting business sufficiently to convince me that he could have set up as a fully qualified bookie if he had been driven to it. Every morning at breakfast the newspaper was opened at the sports page, and the lists and the tipsters' fancies reviewed. It was all Greek to me; but I had only to wait until he had completed his list of possible selections for the " three o'clock " or the

" four o'clock," or whatever it was, at Cheltenham or Folkestone or elsewhere. Then he would say, "Now, Billy, what about a horse for to-day ? " and would read out his lists of names at a great rate. When he came to one called Semiquaver, I cut in with " Half a crown on Semiquaver: that will be sure to go fast." He agreed quite seriously and put something on himself. No one was more surprised than I was when later on in the day we found that it had won.

Sir Edward was a member of the Worcester Race Club and so could go into the enclosure at the Worcester Races. I went with him once or twice and found as much entertainment in watching *him* in this strange and, to me, new environment as in the racing.

I don't know how he got on financially, whether he won or lost. He was always very reserved and mysterious in these matters; but I gathered from things he said from time to time that he managed to lose no more than he could afford for the fun of the sport.

One day when I arrived at Marl Bank I was rushed off to see what they were doing at Worcester, widening the bridge over his beloved Severn: the old familiar bridge he had known all his life. I was taken there so often that I guessed he had something in his head about it. At last it came out. He could not bear to part with the old iron balustrades—or whatever they are called—that were being removed; so he bought two lengths of them and had them brought up on lorries to Marl Bank and set up there on a concrete bed. I thought they looked rather crazy in the garden, but took care not to say so; for he was so delighted when they were set up that we had to go out repeatedly to study them from all points of view and discuss what colour they should be painted. He decided to keep them as like their old selves as possible. I think he used to go out and imagine that the Severn was flowing under them as of old.

This had one musical result: the Severn Suite. It was written for the annual brass-band contest at the Crystal Palace; and was dedicated to Bernard Shaw in recognition of his heroism in going one morning to the Palace and listening to innumerable bands from all over the country blasting their way through the suite one after another until nightfall. The rescoring of this work for full orchestra, and its performance at the Worcester Festival which followed, kept Sir Edward busy for a while. The most popular theme in the Severn Suite is, however, a relic of early days when it was composed and laid aside. This was quickly followed by another new work for orchestra—the Nursery Suite, written for and dedicated to

THEIR ROYAL HIGHNESSES THE DUCHESS OF YORK

AND THE

PRINCESSES ELIZABETH AND MARGARET ROSE.

I remember the first performance of this suite, which took place at the Kingsway Hall, where the orchestra assembled to record it for the Gramophone Company

(H.M.V.). After it had been thoroughly rehearsed and the records made successfully, we were informed that their Royal Highnesses the Duke and Duchess of York had expressed a wish to hear it and that they were coming within a few minutes. Upon their arrival, Mr. Fred Gaisberg (artistic director of the company) handed them each a copy *de luxe* of the score, and we then proceeded to play it under Sir Edward's own direction. When we had played the number " The Wagon Passes," their Royal Highnesses' faces were wreathed in smiles and, at their request, Sir Edward repeated it. At the end of the whole suite they most cordially expressed their appreciation of the music to Sir Edward and also of the way it had been rendered by those performing, and to signify this they requested Sir Edward to present me, as leader of the orchestra on that occasion, to them—a great honour which I can never forget whenever I hear or take part in a performance of this work.

Between times he worked fitfully at the Opera. Meanwhile we walked to exercise the dogs or drove over to Bromsgrove to see his sister Polly (Mrs. Graften) and his nephews and nieces, Roland, Gerald, May, Madge, and Clare, who were all much attached to him; indeed, one or other of them—May in particular, perhaps—was always on a visit at Marl Bank, helping Miss Clifford to look after him and keep him from getting depressed.

For it was at this time that his health began to fail.

He was troubled with nettlerash, a maddening and ridiculous affliction which had to be kept secret, and made it very difficult for him to keep quiet when it was presently complicated by lumbago so severe that at the Hereford Festival of 1930 he had to be helped to the conductor's rostrum, where he *sat* to conduct through the performance and then was helped down again.

Apparently the Festival cured him; for he was soon able to move about actively again. Mrs. Shaw, who urged him to get overhauled by an osteopath, was volcanically rebuffed, and then apologetically warned that she must not suggest unregistered Americans to the King's Master of Music: a typical instance of the strength of his conventional side. He was so vigorous that he allowed Mr. Gaisberg to snatch him over to Paris with Dick (his valet and constant attendant) to conduct the Violin Concerto for Yehudi Menuhin, who played it magnificently, leaving Elgar intensely pleased and thrilled by his performance.

The double journey was made by air: Elgar's first and last experience of flying. He went off smiling, with no qualms, as if he had spent his life in aeroplanes. While in Paris he went to see Delius, who was very ill and nearly blind. The meeting was most cordial. They chatted together and discussed the state of music and the reaction of the present generation to modern ideas as if they were in the habit of having friendly meetings every day. Elgar was very full of it when he came back, having found in Delius a kindred spirit; for Elgar had great difficulty in discussing music with most professional musicians, especially composers.

When the Hereford Festival of 1933 came, I little thought it was to be his last. He took a house for the week, with a convenient garden in front which was daily thronged with people coming to tea. They came in and out, and one hardly knew who they all were; but the Festival spirit prevailed—it was open door and hospitality throughout the week.

Sir Edward, I feel sure, enjoyed it, though he did not move about very much or seem to want to go for walks as before. He sat mostly in that pleasant garden receiving and entertaining his friends when he was not busy rehearsing or conducting. He had the full score of *Elijah* by him and would show Bernard Shaw and others his pet points in it: things which appealed to him and of which he never tired.

He spoke very little of the works of his contemporary composers, especially of the younger school. He liked some of them in a mild sort of way, but none of them gave him such thrills as he derived from the classics or from the Handel oratorios. He retained to the end his love for all the works that appealed to him as a boy. He was a Wagner enthusiast; he adored most of Berlioz and would enjoy at any time looking at the scores of the lesser-known works, such as the Overtures, *The Corsair, Les Francs Juges*, or *Harold in Italy*.

He liked nearly all Schumann, Mendelssohn, Brahms, and some of the older operas by Rossini, Meyerbeer, etc. He was very fond of Puccini's *Tosca*, and would often play portions of it on the piano. He liked all Beethoven, Mozart, and Haydn, and would often sit and read the scores of Haydn's quartets, Mozart's operas, or any of the lesser-known symphonies of any of these composers by way of relaxation. He liked the tone poems of Liszt and most of his followers, and had a great admiration for the works of Richard Strauss.

Generally speaking, he liked all music labelled by some as romantic or lyrical, music with fire and rhythm, music with blood flowing in it, live music. He had very small appreciation for what he termed anæmic music, or music lacking in all, or any, of the above qualities. In much of it he could not see why it should have a beginning or an end; it seemed to him to meander on without any suspicion of a climax, or any feeling that it was working to any definite point, mere *notes* grouped in more or less intricate patterns; characteristically, he described it to me as " a dismal form of entertainment."

As has been said, he retained his juvenile enthusiasms throughout his life. Wagner, perhaps, seemed greater to him than he would seem to future generations. His respect for Berlioz and Liszt may possibly be denounced by the younger generation of musicians as boyish and old-fashioned. But Elgar never stood on the dignity of his tastes: he would speak of Handel

with tears in his eyes, and then send an urgent telegram to Bernard Shaw to insist on his buying at once
a record of "Oh, Mo'nah," a fox-trot played by Jay
Wilbur and his jazz band. One of his pet records was
a song about

> *Mucking around the garden,*
> *Dear old Uncle Joe,*

but pronounced with a north-country accent. Some of
the later jazz records fascinated him to such an extent
that he would put them on his gramophone again and
again. Some twist in the rhythm or daring modulation gave him quite a thrill. He would nod his head
thoughtfully, and say, "Whoever scored and arranged
this is a genius." There was some quite commonplace
song that rambled about aimlessly in various keys
until it seemed to have become quite lost; whoever
was responsible for this was not to be baulked by such
a detail, however, for when the refrain was reached
he switched it back to the original key with the
greatest effrontery. It sounded grotesque and quite
extraordinary, and, although Elgar could not stand
the major portion of the song, he was always turning
this bit on, as he enjoyed the " cheek of it " so much.

None of these things influenced him at all in his
own musical conceptions; they only entertained him.
As will be seen by a study of the fragments he left of his
Third Symphony, he went on progressing as he grew
older, but writing, as ever, entirely in his own way.

PLATE IX : SIR EDWARD WITH BERNARD SHAW AT MISS BARROW'S SCHOOL,
" LAWNSIDE," MALVERN

THEY HAVE JUST BEEN PLAYING PIANO DUETS TO THE LADY IN THE PICTURE,
MRS. CLAUDE BEDDINGTON, WHO WAS ALSO A GUEST AT " LAWNSIDE "

I have been led away from the Hereford garden in 1933 into this general record of his tastes because he talked a good deal about music there to all sorts of people. Now I must get back to the tragic end of my story.

After the Festival, I returned to my normal routine in London, leaving Elgar to wrestle with a godsend in the shape of a munificent commission from Sir John Reith on behalf of the British Broadcasting Corporation for a new symphony to be produced in the following year at a B.B.C. Elgar Festival. He had been working at this intermittently all the year; and I had played many fragments of it for him and watched hopefully as his pile of MS. kept growing.

Suddenly a letter came from Miss Clifford saying she would be glad if I could possibly come, as he had had some sort of bad attack and was staying in bed for a day or two: better, but complaining of a pain like sciatica. I thought it was probably his old enemy lumbago, and was making plans to go down and see whether I could cheer him up a little or do anything to help when I was startled to hear that he was to undergo some small operation and was going into a nursing-home for it at once.

The next thing I heard was that the operation had taken place; that it was far more serious than had at first been supposed; that he was too ill to see anyone for some days, but would like to see me as soon as he could.

All this gave me a cold chill and a feeling of appre-
hension; but I was a little reassured when I received
a postcard which was very characteristic.

The name of the nursing-home was South Bank.
The handwriting on the postcard I received was
Carice's, and the printed heading was as usual Marl
Bank; but he himself had put a pen through Marl,
altered it to South, and added, " But, oh! the
difference to me."

When I went to see him he broke down and wept
piteously. I held his hand tightly in mine for a long
time until he became calmer. At last he said, " Don't
take any notice. I was afraid that, when I saw you,
Billy, I should make a fool of myself." I reassured him
as well as I could. Then he wanted to know: Were
they looking after me properly at Marl Bank? Did
they fetch me from the station? When I had to go
back to London, had they arranged for Dick to meet
me?—and so on. He had forgotten himself and was
only thinking of me. He said he knew how busy I was,
and how he thought it so good of me to come all that
way to see him, and a good deal more in the same
strain until I nearly wept in my turn.

When I went back to Marl Bank in the evening
Carice told me that his doctor, Dr. Moore-Ede—son
of the Dean of Worcester—was coming to see me.
I thought this very unusual. My heart sank; and
I dreaded this meeting.

We had dinner. It seemed terrible dining there

without Sir Edward and thinking of him in the nursing-home.

Soon after dinner, Dr. Moore-Ede came, and my worst fears were almost realised. He told me he knew that I was Elgar's nearest and most intimate friend and must therefore be told the truth.

The operation was only a temporary measure, no good as a cure; for the trouble was malignant, and the only thing that could be done was to try to alleviate the pain. If the growth could be kept inactive he might perhaps get well enough to come home. He might even regain sufficient strength to finish the symphony for the B.B.C.

I said, " Do you mean that his days are numbered, and that it is impossible for him to get well again and be his old self ? " The doctor nodded his head sadly. He might live for six months, perhaps a year or more; but that was the most he could give me to hope for. In any case, he said, he must gradually fail and always be more or less an invalid.

We agreed that this state of affairs must not get into the newspapers, as Sir Edward would see it and that would upset him. He liked to read every day that he was " progressing favourably."

One morning, when I arrived at the nursing-home, he said with a strained expression, " Have you seen ? They say I am not going to get better ! "

I reassured him by saying that the bulletin meant " for some time." Lord Horder had been and examined him a day or two before, and had said that everything that could be done for him was being done, meaning that nothing could be done to avert the final catastrophe. Meanwhile, the patient had much pain. Something was pressing on the sciatic nerve; and he had very bad periods, which wore him down.

Also, happily, there were times when the pain died down, and he could sleep peacefully and then wake refreshed and quite cheerful.

His brain was active as ever. He could talk eagerly about his beloved Teme Valley. When he was better we were to explore it together.

He rarely said anything about the symphony; but I knew he had not forgotten it, though I naturally refrained from talking about it—unless he mentioned it himself—for fear of distressing him.

So I went back to London, where almost daily a letter or postcard came to say he had had a very bad night, but was better, or he was brighter and more cheerful.

I went to and fro as often as I could, wondering as the days went on whether he would ever be well enough physically to sit up and write down the notes in a long full score. The mental effort, I thought, he *could* make; for I felt he had already worked out in his mind the greater part of the symphony; but I feared very much that his bodily strength would never again stand the arduous strain of sitting hour after hour laboriously setting it down in black and white.

When he was well enough to dictate, I offered to act as his amanuensis, only to realise that he could never stand the strain of such work again.

So the symphony remained so incomplete that none of it can ever be played, and, as will be seen later, he left instructions that the task of trying to complete it was never to be attempted.

On the morning of November 20th, 1933, I received this telegram: " Father unconscious, sinking rapidly —My love—CARICE." After the first shock, which seemed to numb my senses, I gradually realised its import, and, as its full meaning grew on me, hastened to the telephone. Yes; he was still unconscious and his doctor could not hold out much hope, but, just before he passed into this state, he was asking for me. Could I come—as he might rally during the day? I hurriedly looked up the next train to Worcester. What time did it leave Paddington, and could I catch it?

I arrived at Worcester in the early afternoon, and was driven at once to the nursing-home, where Sir Edward was lying still unconscious, but, as was whispered to me, showing signs of improvement. I sat watching him for some time, noting his familiar features. They had scarcely changed during his illness: his hair was a little whiter perhaps, and his characteristic nose, with its high bridge, a trifle more prominent; but his colour was good, and he did not look very much thinner than before.

While I was letting my mind run back over the

Hн   113

thirty or more years during which he had honoured me with his closest friendship, he suddenly opened his eyes, and, looking intently into my face for a few seconds, uttered my name, as a smile stole over his face. Closing his eyes, he seemed to lapse once more into unconsciousness, and I exchanged some whispered words with his daughter Carice and the nurse, both of whom were also watching. Presently he stirred again, and, putting out his hand, let it rest on mine, and drew me a little nearer. Silence, except for the ticking of the clock and an occasional settling down of the coal in the fireplace. Then it was evident that he was trying very hard to speak; and gradually and at long intervals the words came from him. " I want you . . . to do something for me . . . the symphony all bits and pieces . . . no one would understand . . . no one . . . no one."

A look of great anguish came over his face as he said this, and his voice died away from exhaustion. Leaning over him, I said, "What can I do for you ? Try to tell me. I will do anything for you; you know that."

Again a long silence; but a more peaceful expression came back into his face, and before long he drew me down again and said, "Don't let anyone tinker with it . . . no one could understand . . . no one must tinker with it."

I assured him that no one would ever tamper with it in any way, or attempt to construct what would have to be a most unsatisfactory work. In fact, it was quite impossible to bring any one of the four movements which were all " bits and pieces " into shape, even with the best intentions, without relying principally on guesswork, and inserting a very large quantity of more or less new and unauthentic stuff to bind all the genuine fragments together. A little while later he said in a whisper and with great emotion, " I think you had better burn it."

I exchanged glances with his daughter, who was now sitting at the opposite side of the bed; and I saw that she looked, as I am sure I did, a little startled at this suggestion. Then I felt that it was only a suggestion and not really a request; so I leaned over him and said, "I don't think it is necessary to burn it: it would be awful to do that. But Carice and I will remember that no one is to try to put it together. No one shall ever tinker with it: we promise you that."

Hearing this, he seemed to grow more peaceful. His strugglings and efforts to speak ceased; he lay there with his eyes open, watching us, and seemed quite content.

From that day, he rallied and improved so much that it became possible to move him to his home at Marl Bank early in the New Year. I began to see visions of his ultimate recovery; and, though I anticipated that he would always be an invalid, I thought it just possible that he would be able to take up the threads of his Third Symphony after all, and even muster enough health and strength to finish it. But this was not to be. In his own home he slowly but surely slipped downhill. I went there constantly from London, and it was pitiful to see him receding, fading away from us all so certainly that there was no doubt about the hopelessness of his illness. The only wonder was that he fought so long and so patiently before he left us finally on February 23rd, 1934.

He never again referred to his symphony; he seemed quite resigned to the thought that it would never be finished, and I always feel that he knew no one would ever " tinker with it."

There was one incident that cheered him tremendously before he died.

I went one morning to his room and found him propped up on his pillows, his eyes shining with excitement over a letter in his hand he had just read. It was from Mr. Fred Gaisberg to say that he was making some records shortly, and was wondering if Sir Edward would be able to take part in the recording, even though confined to his bed.

If he were well enough and the doctors would allow it, the Gramophone Company would fix a loudspeaker and a microphone in his room, so that he could hear, direct, everything that was taking place at the recording-studio at St. John's Wood in London when they were at work on *Caractacus*.

He was very excited about this suggestion; and I saw that he must on no account be disappointed. He had not to move in order to speak; in fact, no physical effort was needed; so his doctor consented to let him make this attempt.

I went back to London and telephoned to Mr. Gaisberg at once. A date was agreed upon; the London Symphony Orchestra was engaged; and Mr. Gaisberg went to Worcester to make final arrangements. Dick (Sir Edward's valet) made an ingenious music-stand which went across the bed so that the full scores would be in a good position for Sir Edward to see without effort; the microphone position was fixed; and contact was made by land-lines to London. The day was fixed for January 22nd, 1934; and, as this day grew nearer, Sir Edward had some very bad turns which made the project seem quite hopeless at times. Even on the appointed morning he seemed to be only half conscious. But he suddenly recovered complete consciousness before the arranged time (four in the afternoon); and he was quite lucid and able to direct the proceedings from his bed. Fred Gaisberg was there with him, Dick also, to move the stand or make adjustments if necessary. At the Abbey Road studio the London Symphony Orchestra had assembled at two o'clock to rehearse the Triumphal March and woodland scenes from *Caractacus*—Lawrance Collingwood conducting. Exactly at four o'clock, silence was called, and the microphone became " alive." Rex Palmer spoke from the studio to Sir Edward, Mr. Gaisberg, Carice, and some others who were admitted —at Sir Edward's wish—to his room at Marl Bank.

Sir Edward asked who was there; and then I went to the microphone at Abbey Road and told him that all his best bandsmen were there and sent their loves; also Lawrance Collingwood. I gave several names, and described where they were sitting, so that he had a mental picture of the orchestra at work.

Then there was a fearful crackling of the loud speaker. When this subsided, Sir Edward's voice was heard, welcoming the players, the conductor, and the others assembled. He said, "I am afraid my voice is rather like an old crow; but I hope you can all hear what I say." Then he asked us to play over what we had been rehearsing; and when this was done he criticised it from his bed—too fast here—the clarinet must come out more there—the flute—the oboe—the strings: he had some little hint to give about all these matters. He listened to the actual recording after the trials had been made, and expressed himself well satisfied with the afternoon's work, just as if he had been at the studio in person.

The music-stand which Dick made to hold the scores is now in the care of Mr. Gaisberg, who keeps it as a treasured possession, this being the last music-stand Sir Edward used and the last time he recorded.

Mr. Gaisberg's idea in arranging for that last recording was to help Elgar in his severe illness, and to let him feel that he was still in contact with the world at large; the gramophone was his solace throughout his illness, and he was always asking for his favourite records to be put on, both at the nursing-home and after he was taken back to Marl Bank. He never tired of listening, and he always enjoyed the actual recording; it is hardly necessary to say that he was greeted with the greatest affection and esteem by everyone in the company whenever he went to the studio to take up the baton.

Sir Edward had begun to record his works for the Gramophone Company about the year 1910, but it was not until 1914 that he signed his first contract with this company, the event being brought about by Landon Ronald (now Sir Landon), who introduced him to Mr. Alfred Clark, the managing director of His Master's Voice Gramophone Company, by which name this firm was then known. In the first three months of 1915 he recorded *Pomp and Circumstance* March (No. 4 in G), the Bavarian Dances, and *Carillon*, the music he wrote for the poem by Emile Cammaerts—Mr. Henry Ainley recited the poem on this occasion.

Just after nine o'clock in the morning of Friday, February 23rd, 1934, a telegram came to me from Worcester: " End came most peacefully 7.45 this morning—Please tell Gaisberg—Love." I went to the telephone and carried out this instruction; then returned dully and tried to go on with my work as before. I found this impossible. I was roused and brought to my senses by a telephone call from Sir

Ivor Atkins from Worcester. He was coming at once to London to see me.

Now, if there is one sympathetic soul in this world—especially in our love and profound veneration for Elgar—it is Ivor Atkins; and I lived for the minute when he should arrive. It was a great relief when he came. My pent-up feelings could be freed: we could commune together over our loss, and say things, in the friendship we shared for the great man, which were not for the whole world to hear. Ivor Atkins had known him for more years than I had, though we forbear to argue about the closeness of our respective friendships: it is enough for us that they existed.

Sir Ivor wanted a memorial service in Worcester Cathedral at once, before the funeral if possible; but the time was too short for this, as the funeral took place on the following Monday. I went down and stayed with Sir Ivor on the Sunday, and we attended the burial service at St. Wulstan's, Little Malvern, on the morning of February 26th. Sir Ivor, Sir Landon Ronald, Troyte Griffiths, Mary Clifford, Hubert Leicester, his son Philip, Dick, and myself were the only followers outside his own family. This was in fulfilment of his desire very definitely expressed to Carice during his last days.

It was fortunate for Sir Ivor and for me that immediate action on our part was imperative. We had to confer and arrange all details for the memorial service in the cathedral. Sir Ivor had Friday, March 2nd, in

PLATE X : ELGAR AS A CYCLIST

view; but we had first to find whether we could assemble the London Symphony Orchestra, the soloists, and the Festival Choir on that day.

Sir Ivor took infinite pains, in making the programme, to select suitable excerpts from Sir Edward's works. The cathedral was full. Eminent musicians, from all over the country, who could get there in time were present; and the service proved to be one of the most—if not *the* most—impressive services that have ever taken place in Worcester Cathedral. The orchestral players and the solo singers came all the way from London freely, giving up any private work they may have had, only too eager to pay their tribute of deep respect to the memory of this great musician.

The choir and Sir Ivor himself were beyond praise; they gave all they had with tears in their eyes. And so the service ended as it had begun, on a note of sublime and serene simplicity. This, then, was the prelude to another act of homage which Sir Ivor had conceived—he wished for something permanent and visible to perpetuate the long association of the great Worcester musician with the cathedral. He wanted an Elgar memorial window to be set over the spot by the pillar where Elgar was always to be found listening during the Festival performances.

This idea was caught up, and the means were at once forthcoming. The window was entrusted to Mr. A. K. Nicholson, who carried out a conception based upon *The Dream of Gerontius*.

The unveiling of this window took place on the opening day of the Worcester Festival, September 3rd, 1935. The Bishop of the Diocese and the Dean of Worcester, and Viscount Cobham as Lord Lieutenant, with the conductors of the Three Choirs, and others, proceeded to the window for the dedication.

Here is the order of the ceremony as printed:

" The Dean will request the Lord Lieutenant to unveil the window, and, this done, there shall follow:

" Equale for Trombones (Beethoven).

" The music ended, the Dean, turning to the Bishop, shall say: ' Reverend Father, we ask you to dedicate this Window to the Glory of God, humbly trusting that its painted glass may through succeeding generations enshrine the memory of Edward Elgar, an illustrious musician.'

" The Bishop will then offer the Window to Almighty God in these words: ' To the Glory of God and in memory of Edward Elgar we dedicate this Window, in the name of the Father, and of the Son, and of the Holy Ghost. Amen.' Then shall follow, from the works of Elgar, Variation 9 (Nimrod) of the Enigma Variations.

" The music ended, the Bishop and Clergy, with the Lord Lieutenant and those with them, will return to their places and the oratorio, *The Dream of Gerontius*, will begin."

The Worcester Corporation have now purchased the cottage at Broadheath where Elgar was born; and here many of his personal effects, his desk, his pens, etc., can be seen by those who make the pilgrimage.

In conclusion, it is comforting to feel that one does not have to say "Farewell"; for, though the physical Elgar has passed from us, the spiritual Elgar remains enshrined in his works—a glorious heritage.

PART II

ELGAR THE COMPOSER

ELGAR THE COMPOSER

IT IS ALWAYS INTERESTING and not a little surprising to hear the comments of people who are supposed to be " musical " when they enter upon a discussion of a composer or his work. " I don't do anything at music, but I am a good listener," they say,
and then proceed to appraise the work of a great man,
sometimes rapturously and sometimes scathingly.

If a composer stopped to think what effect the work
he was creating was likely to have upon others, he
would in all likelihood never achieve anything of
artistic value or permanence. He must express himself
and his own personal feelings with an entire disregard
for the susceptibilities of others.

If he is really true to himself in this respect, his
personality is inevitably stamped upon his work, so
that whether, like Berlioz, he is writing for five
hundred performers, or a study for one soloist—composing an oratorio or a part song, a symphony or a
drawing-room piece for violin and piano—the listener immediately says, "That is Bach, or Brahms, or
Beethoven, or Grieg, or—Elgar."

No composer has more surely stamped his own indi-
viduality upon his work than Elgar. There is in it

127

something intangible. I cannot define it; but it is something arresting which holds the listener in thrall.

There are people who do not like Elgar's music, even when they have become used to his idiom; but they have to acknowledge its power. It may be that the very strength of the underlying personality is the cause of their antipathy, just as this same strength is the attraction for others. In any case, they are held. No one can listen to Elgar's music with complete indifference, whether it is *The Dream of Gerontius*, *The Apostles*, or *After many a Dusty Mile* set for male voices from the Greek Anthology.

The people who " do not do anything at music, but are good listeners," are naturally curious as to how this phenomenon, this crystallisation of a composer's own personality in the form of crotchets and quavers, can be brought about. If it *could* be explained, everyone could do it, and the world would teem with genius; but the composer himself has not the remotest idea how or why it comes to him, any more than we can explain why our handwritings differ. We only know that one handwriting has character, and another very little: this one is pompous and bumptious, that one timid, weak, and insipid, and the other merely common.

I once asked Elgar how he produced that terrifying sound in *The Apostles* when Judas goes out and hangs himself. How did he catch that significant sound and get it on paper in ordinary musical symbols? He could not tell me. He just saw Judas in the extremity of his remorse putting what he hoped would be an end to himself, and *heard* it on the muted horn conveying unerringly the full horror of the situation. He always said that music is "written on the sky," implying that the inspired composer has nothing to do but copy it.

What was Elgar's actual method ? Did he sit down and say to himself, "Now I will write a symphony, or a string quartet," or did he get a book of poems and search for something to set to music ?

He did none of these things. He had no method, in the ordinarily accepted sense of the term. He conceived his music at all times—in the middle of the night, out walking, in a crowd, or in solitude—scribbling his ideas on any piece of paper that came handy, to be noted more fully on music paper and considered from all possible points of view in various keys and in varying moods. Like Beethoven, he allowed an idea, which may have occurred to him as a short phrase, to germinate and transform and throw out branches. He rarely started anything at the beginning. He worked at a theme and brought it perhaps to a climax; for then, as he has said to me, he knew to what he was leading.

Often there would come to him ideas which had nothing to do with the particular work upon which he was engaged at the time. He would note them down, however; and they would find a place later on, in another movement, perhaps, or even in a totally different work.

When we were looking through some of these notes one day, and came across a tune with the word " Tuba " written over it, he told me that if he thought of any instrument's tone quality he would naturally invent music proper to it. Hence this particular tune was labelled " Tuba," as it came to him when he was considering the timbre and sonority of that instrument.

On looking at this fragment in his scrap-book more closely, I thought it seemed strangely familiar; I then realised that he had used it as the principal subject of the Finale in his Second Symphony.

It is still more strange to note, however, that he did not give this tune to the tuba after all; it is true that the tuba makes rhythmic comments upon it a few bars after 138 and plays a fragment of it at 149, also after 159, but this is all he allows this instrument—meagre fare when anticipating a full meal.

He wrote innumerable repetitions of the same section in the music; I have seen a matter of twenty or thirty bars written in short score eight or nine times

PLATE XI : ELGAR WITH MENUHIN IN PARIS

without very much change except for a little twist here or an interpolation there. He liked to see how it shaped—how it presented itself to the eye as well as to the ear. Fugitive phrases he would redraft and play with by inversion, augmentation, and other devices as if they haunted him.

He made great use of sequences, both real and tonal; and this has been pointed out as a weakness by some people, but he handled them with such mastery that he made them seem inevitable.

Who could cavil at the sequence beginning at the eighteenth bar of *Gerontius*, with its four repetitions; or at the one in *The Apostles* ("In the mountain— Night"), starting at Fig. 15 (*mistico*)? Observe what has been done with this idea which sets out so quietly, keeps appearing and reappearing throughout the work, and then becomes so hair-raising and terrific at "All the ends of the world shall remember" (Fig. 233), which is sung *tutta forza* by the choir.

His works abound in sequences and sequential writing, but there is always something distinctive and personal about them, something belonging entirely to himself, and not at all reminiscent of any other composer. Look at the opening bars of *Falstaff*! This looks like a real sequence; but on examination it is seen that the first interval is a perfect fourth. It is imitated in the first repetition as a diminished fourth, and in the next as a diminished fifth. The minor third and perfect fifth persist for two bars, and are altered to a diminished fourth and a perfect fifth at the third repetition. A bar is then interpolated (fourth bar), but with such a curious twist that it makes the next three bars sound differently in the ear, in spite of the fact that they are nearly a repetition of the opening phrase except for the little *codetta*.

The *contrafagotto* which touches up the bass notes from the fourth bar onwards, assisted by the double basses, who play the same notes *pizzicato* on the odd beats, of course help to create the illusion that there is something different about this repetition; but they have added nothing to the score harmonically: they have only solidified the bass and given the phrase rhythmic emphasis.

The Music Makers opens with a sequential theme which goes downward in two-bar curves twice and then proceeds in one-bar curves three times repeated until the initial note C is reached an octave lower. At Fig. 2 (*tranquillo e cantabile*) we are introduced to another sequential theme, beginning on A rising in two-bar curves four times repeated to C a tenth above the initial note. These two themes serve practically for the whole of the Prelude; but the contrast between the two is so pronounced—the mood of the first being agitated and rather turbulent, while the second is restful and comforting—that no feeling of monotony is produced: quite the contrary; for the Prelude as a whole is noble and uplifting.

Another characteristic of Elgar's music is his habit

of repeating a short figure or phrase of two notes (a dotted crotchet followed by a quaver) any number of times in the construction of one of his themes. See, for instance, the principal theme in the *allegro* in the last movement of the First Symphony, sixteen bars (i.e. thirty-two repetitions) before a change is made four bars before (Fig. 113), and even the violins carry it on for four more bars (*legato*). In the Second Symphony (first movement, Fig. 1) we have a crotchet followed by a quaver repeated four times in each bar for eight bars (again thirty-two repetitions). In the Finale of this symphony an examination of the structure of the second subject (Fig. 139) reveals again this rhythmic device

but using dotted quaver semiquavers, instead of dotted crotchet quavers, making six repetitions in every two bars, but accumulating energy each time, so that it provides a strong impact at the third bar of the theme.

Again in the unfinished Third Symphony this same characteristic appears. The second subject of the first movement has the dotted crotchet followed by a quaver persisting as in his earlier works.

The principal subject in the first movement of the 'Cello Concerto has the same figuration as the principal subject in the first movement of the Second Symphony, only in triple time instead of quadruple, making three repetitions in each bar instead of four.

133

In spite of this, curiously enough, there is no resemblance whatever in the effect produced upon the mind by these two themes so similar on paper, so dissimilar in effect. In the symphony the theme is buoyant, swinging along energetically, full of fire and lively to a degree. In the 'Cello Concerto the effect is dreamy and meditative, thoughtful and serene. Yet both these themes consist of a crotchet followed by a quaver persistently repeated. The moral surely is that crotchets and quavers in themselves mean nothing: they are only the vehicle that carries the composer's intention. The underlying meaning of the music is all that matters, and Elgar, a master of his craft, could take any phrase and weave round it a web of sound which would charge it with any feeling the human mind is capable of experiencing.

One of his most original strokes, and one that is lost on those who listen perfunctorily with semi-detached minds, is the recitation of the Beatitudes in a movement named " By the Wayside " in *The Apostles*. In this we hear Jesus, Mary Magdalene, and the disciples, walking along conversing in the most natural manner. I do not think there is any other music in existence which achieves this miracle. The writing is simplicity itself; yet such is its power that we can actually visualise the characters walking, and turning to one another as they speak. Their personalities are expressed too: the sinister chord that accompanies Judas when he sings, " The rich hath many friends," gives us a

cold shiver and leaves us in no doubt as to the state
of his mind, his envy of rich people, and his ultimate
fate. The actual harmony and the way it is orchestrated
convey this with great sureness.

This power of Elgar to delineate character in terms
of musical sound is apparent in many of his works, the
Enigma Variations being the outstanding example.
" Dedicated to my friends pictured within " is
inscribed on the original score.

In *Falstaff* the actual characters, and in *Cockaigne*
the imaginary ones, are clearly portrayed. It is this
same power which enabled him to convert into
musical phrase and texture the ordinary incidents of
life, as well as the whole range of emotions, the subtleties, and all those deeper things, most of which cannot
be expressed in words at all.

Examples of these subtleties can be found in all his
works. Occasionally he writes suggestions, such as
" Smiling with a sigh," on his MS.; but mostly he lets
the music speak for itself.

Who can describe in words the infinite yearning and
tenderness contained in such a phrase as this from
Gerontius—or the music that is written for the words

" Oh, what a heart-subduing melody," or the passage set to the words " And bid them come to thee. . . .
To that Glorious Home "—also from *Gerontius*, quoted

in *The Music Makers* (Fig. 101) *after* the soloist has
sung, " And a singer who sings no more," the choir
entering at the fourth bar of the phrase with the
reiteration " No more " ? Also Mary Magdalene's
music in *The Apostles* : what could be more pathetic
than these halting phrases between Figs. 84 and 86—
" My tears run down like a river " ? Their deep
feeling is inexpressible except in music.

Not only the deeper feelings, but humour, lightness,
gaiety are all faithfully recorded in his works. The
very opening theme in *Falstaff* has a broadly humorous
flavour, especially when it is used later to depict the
hero in his cups, or composing himself to sleep. That
this same theme, however, in the hands of genius is

136

capable of expressing all things may be seen by noting the pathos in its last halting appearance at Fig. 145, near the end of the work, when Sir John lies dying.

The solo on the muted side-drum which follows leaves one spellbound at the sureness of touch and the instinct for orchestral effect shown by Elgar.

It goes without saying that it cost him no effort to make clever and genuine fun with the trombone and percussion in such episodes as " The Wild Bears " in the first suite from *The Wand of Youth*, and his imagination is shown very plainly in " The Tame Bears." Here the clumsy shuffling of the dancing bear is depicted unmistakably, and the effect is enhanced by the rattling of the chain so cleverly indicated by the cymbals, tambourine, etc. The little interlude between the repetition of the principal theme is evidently the half-frightened, excited movements of the onlookers as the animal lurches towards them. But, in spite of this facility, Elgar very rarely describes incidents in his music; he is much more concerned at creating an atmosphere. He can unerringly convey a sense of glamour or pageantry as in *The Crown of India*, *Falstaff*, *In the South*, and the Overture, *Cockaigne*, *The Kingdom*, *Pomp and Circumstance* Marches; or solemnity in the opening bars of *The Apostles*; or daintiness and delicacy in *The Wand of Youth* Suite, with its opening march and its " Moth and Butterflies," and the first movement of the little Serenade for Strings. The slow movement of the Second Symphony and the great moment in *Gerontius* marked *moderato e solenne* (Fig. 18) speak for themselves and show to what sublime heights Elgar could rise.

There is a magical wistfulness in Falstaff's dream of his boyhood as page to the Duke of Norfolk. The music describes no incident, but gives, to perfection, the inexplicable sadness—by no means melancholy—of dreaming of one's youthful days.

How wistful too is the theme played by the solo quartet at the opening of the *allegro* in the Introduction and Allegro for Strings! I feel almost sure, in thinking about it, that it was over these bars that Elgar wrote " Smiling with a sigh."

Mysticism was a very strong trait in Elgar; it came out in all he did, and of course found its way into his music. Countless examples could be given; but perhaps this quality was more apparent in *The Dream of Gerontius* than in any other of his works. Let me quote one supreme example from this work, one of the most mystical pieces of writing—*the* most mystical, perhaps—in all the realm of music. On p. 86 in the full score, at the third bar after Fig. 12 in Part II, the angel sings, " Alleluia for evermore "; but what has happened to the orchestra? It is upside down: the melody is in the double basses at a remote distance from the voice and the second violins, four octaves apart, as though we had lost touch entirely with the world as we know it, and could not find the usual dimensions.

This passage occurs once more between Figs. 15 and 16; but now it accompanies the words "Alleluia, from earth to heaven"; and these words, "From earth to heaven," are surely the key to this daring piece of writing.

The passage is in three parts; and the distribution of the notes, with the bass and treble in consecutive octaves and the parts widely separated, should sound atrocious according to the text-books; but in performance it sounds perfectly astonishing, producing in the minds of the listeners an uncertain feeling of dimension, and a sense of remoteness from any earthly contact.

Not far removed from this vein of mysticism is the intense *spirituality* of so much of the music of Elgar.

This is no place to discuss creeds or religions, or what he believed and what he did not. The fact is incontrovertible that he has more of that quality which we call—for want of a better word—spirituality than perhaps any other composer.

One can open the pages of almost any of his works— oratorios, symphonies, or short works like *For the Fallen* or *Go, Song of Mine*—to find this quality evident and unmistakable.

Many of his themes too have great dignity. I have often heard cavilling remarks about his habit of marking such passages "*Nobilmente*." Well, why should not he indicate that what he felt and meant to be noble music must be played in a noble manner? He was under no delusion about it: he was a man singularly free from delusions of any kind about anything, extremely clear-headed and quick of perception. When he wrote noble music he was not in the least ashamed to label it. It was only necessary to sit under his baton when he was conducting, and see the seraphic expression which stole over his face when he came to one of these *nobilmente* passages, to realise how he felt. *How* he used to draw himself up and square his shoulders ! He was already a tall man; but at such moments he added several inches to his stature. And what an indescribable expression came into his face as he heard this music soaring and intensifying as it approached one of his many great climaxes !

Elgar was always very reticent and unwilling to discuss the inner meaning of anything he had composed. There was nothing he disliked more. He would change the subject abruptly, or retire into his inner self with some such observation as " Oh, I don't know anything about music. Let us go out and see the river, or go up to the common, and do something sensible for once."

Occasionally, though, he let things slip out when he was taken unawares or worked up by the music itself. I remember once when we were rehearsing the First Symphony, and the passage at Fig. 66 in the second movement was being played in too matter-of-fact a manner to please him, he stopped and said, " Don't play it like that: play it like "—then he hesitated, and

added under his breath, before he could stop himself—
" like something we hear down by the river "—I

never can play or hear that phrase but I am with him
" down by the river " again as I have been so many
times.

Another thing, he hated any of his music to be
played in a rigid manner : he was always asking for it
to be more elastic—only he invariably pronounced it
" elarstic," as it sounded to me, who am also a west-
countryman.

He was very particular about the observance of the
numerous marks of expression, phrasing, pauses,
allargandos, etc., with which he peppered his scores.
He positively disliked seeing any phrase or set of notes
in a bar " naked " as he expressed it. One of the notes
had to be marked with an accent (**>**) or a stress
mark (**—**) or a hairpin (<)(>) *cres.* or *dim.* Something
must happen somewhere or he would deem the
passage " tame."

The sign *fp* occurs very often in his works and he
was very particular about this effect, especially in
Part II of *Gerontius* : one bar after Fig. 20 on the word
" moment."

In *The Kingdom,* one bar after Fig. 146 in the section named " The Arrest," the following direction appears: *pp* ⎯⎯⎯⎯ *pppp subito.* This he always rehearsed more than once; he wanted more *crescendo* in the brass instruments rising to *fff* and then coming off, leaving the strings, bass, and side-drum *pppp* suddenly. After the second or third repetition by the orchestra, when he was apparently satisfied, he invariably said the same thing in the same words (I always knew it was coming and could have said it for him): " Ah ! *now* it is right. I have *never* heard that before: it is the first time it has been properly played."

In those phrases built up of uneven notes ♩. ♪♩. ♪ of which he was so fond, he was always very insistent that the quaver should have its due meed of strength, and I have heard him call out many times during the rehearsals, " Don't starve the quaver "— this was one of his pet expressions. If the performance did not even then reach his standard of perfection, he would stop the orchestra and say he wanted " good old-fashioned bowing"—whatever that may have been —and, fitting the action to the word, give a most surprising and " stylish " demonstration with an imaginary violin and bow, with terrific flourishes quite in the manner of the old days when he and Charles Hayward played in this picturesque way.

Having roused the orchestra to the necessary enthusiasm, he would beam upon them with a seraphic

PLATE XII: ELGAR AND THE AUTHOR IN THE GARDEN AT MARL
BANK WITH MARCO, MINA AND BRIDGET (CARICE'S CAIRN)

smile of satisfaction, though this gradually faded and changed to dismay as he realised that the furore he had provoked was too loud by far for any merely mortal choir, singer, or solo instrument to be heard through; so he had—with a fleeting touch of irritability—to hush the orchestra down, and restrain the ardour he himself had aroused, in order to give the vocalist a chance.

He hated doing this, and insisted that it was the feebleness of the choir or soloist, or anyone, in fact, who could not o'ertop the din when a *fortissimo* was in question.

To return to his characteristic musical idiom—I wonder whether many of his listeners have noticed one more idiosyncratic feature among the many in his work?

It is difficult to describe; but I refer to his habit of taking a note or two, or even a single note, and sounding those same notes innumerable times unchanged in pitch, but changing colour continually as they merged into fresh combinations of the harmonising instruments. He does this very often—in most of his works, in fact. A few examples suffice. In the Second Symphony, first movement (Fig. 23), he has the octave D eight times struck on the harp. The oboe at the fifth stroke joined by the clarinet at the sixth, not only reinforce the tone, but change the colour, just as a skilful painter can change or even create a colour by putting another colour or group of colours beside it. This effect, with different instrumentation, is repeated at Fig. 62.

Sometimes, as in the First Symphony, he takes two notes, Fig. 26, and hammers this little figure out *ff* six times in ten bars, dropping down a note lower at the eleventh bar, amplifying it at Fig. 27, altering the interval, but never letting it go really until Fig. 28.

This little figure appears again four bars before 41, and is again repeated seven times before a slight modification in the notation takes place.

The persistence of the note B♭ (in the lower harmony) all through the section Fig. 66 in the Scherzo, no matter what happens to the melody, is remarkable too; and it happens again after Fig. 77, when a harmonically irrelevant B♭ persists like something thrumming. Then the F♯, which stands out from 87 onwards until it finally settles down at 90, though it changes its colour by passing from one set of instruments to another, yet asserts itself to the end and even becomes the first note of the Adagio which follows.

The two notes E♭ and A♭ used for the *shofar* in the first part of *The Apostles* is another instance, and one after Elgar's own heart, as these two notes, being the actual notes of the ram's horn sounded in the Temple, are unalterable.

How he must have enjoyed scoring this passage with the muted horns and the piccolo tam-tam (little gong) drumming out that interminable E♭, reckless of what any of the other instruments are doing with their B♮ and F♭ in the lower part of the orchestra !

What a tragedy that he never could be induced to write Part III of the Trilogy, where, as he many times told me, this same *shofar* was to sound the Last Trumpet.

Bertram B. Benas, a celebrated writer for the *Jewish Chronicle*, in a letter (dated April 30th, 1934) to Sir Edward Elgar's daughter on the subject (of her father's scholarship in matters of Hebrew music), said :

" I am deeply moved by your mention of the *extreme care* Sir Edward took, in respect of the susceptibilities of my community, in dealing with some of our liturgical melodies—a sentiment so appealing to us in these days so trying and difficult, and, if I may be permitted, I should like to let the editor see that, that he can have the best testimony of the wonderful sympathy of your illustrious father."

Mr. Benas wrote an article entitled "Some Jewish Musical Contacts of the late Sir Edward Elgar," in

the course of which he quoted a note written by
Elgar himself, as follows:

"It has long been my wish to compose an
oratorio which should embody the calling of the
Apostles, their teaching (schooling), and their mis-
sion, culminating in the establishment of the Church
among the Gentiles. . . . The ancient Hebrew
melody (Ps. xcii), commencing on p. 21 (of the
vocal score published by Novellos') is quoted, by
kind permission of the publishers (Messrs. Augener.
& Co.), from the volume by Ernest Pauer, whose
broad and appropriate harmony is retained in a
few bars."

Mr. Benas goes on to tell us that this is a well-
known Sephardic melody, to be found in the recently
published volume of Sephardic synagogue music, also
in the old and new edition of *The Voice of Prayer and
Praise*, published under the auspices of the United
Synagogue.

Closely related to the examples given earlier is the
repetition of a figure as seen in the String Quartet at
Fig. 25, where the second violin repeats

twenty times with slight variations of the actual
notes, and again at Fig. 33; also, in the Finale of the

Sonata for Violin and Pianoforte, commencing at
the top of p. 27 in the piano score, we find at Fig. 43:

first in the pianoforte part, and then taken by the
violin with slight modifications as the music flows
through twelve consecutive repetitions of this figure.
This happens again later on in the movement (Fig.
52) and continues for twelve bars as before. One
would expect this to produce monotony, but it has
not that effect for a moment: on the contrary, it has
a soothing, comforting effect, with its smooth, swinging pulsation. One does not always want something
exciting to be happening: it is very restful to sit
down calmly at times and do nothing in particular
for a short space, without boredom; and this is precisely the effect these figure repetitions produce on the
listener, a reposeful mood of calm contentment.

When I first visited Elgar at his home in Hereford,
he had an Æolian harp, of which he was very fond,
in the crack of a partly opened window, so that the
breeze blowing across the strings set them in vibration.
This produced a shimmering musical sound of elfin
quality, the strings being tuned to concordant intervals; therefore the effect, when the velocity of the

wind varied and swept across the strings, was entrancing.

All the resultant harmonics and overtones rose and fell as the wind pressure changed; sometimes rising to extreme heights, and then falling rapidly if the wind dropped suddenly. One never knew what it was going to do next. The variety and delicacy of the tone were indescribably beautiful: almost inaudible at one moment, then swelling out to intensity in the next. Altogether, it was most fascinating; and Elgar never tired of listening to its fairylike improvisations.

His inexhaustible internal fund of music was very susceptible to suggestion from any external sound, except that of composed music. The lilt of a line of poetry; "what one hears down by the river"; or this Æolian harp—all these things leaped into music in his mind. Æolian harp passages abound in his works. I can always hear these delicate rising harmonics in No. I of the *Sea Pictures* at the words "like violins." In the Introduction and Allegro for Strings, when the *tremolo* in the violins begins against the second subject-tune in the quartet, the *crescendo* and *diminuendo* in the *tremolo* give an exact impression of the minstrelsy of that harp in the window.

Much the same effect is produced by those widely extended chords shimmering in the divided strings (*ppp*) in *Gerontius*, beginning at the fourth bar after Fig. 25 at the words "strange innermost abandonment," and again two bars later. The orchestral harp thrumming the repeated notes in triplets is really an Æolian harp.

In the first movement of the Violin Sonata the *arpeggios* in the second page of the violin part rise and fall—dwelling on a note here and another one there (*tenuto*). When playing or listening to this section of the movement, or its repetitions later on, I always hear the rise and fall of the wind over the strings of a harp.

Elgar was extremely modest about his music; but he was rather proud, and rightly so, of his prodigious skill in laying it out for the orchestra. He knew unerringly what he wanted in the way of orchestral or choral tone, balance, and colour. I do not think he ever altered or modified any single note of anything he had once set down in the score. Meyerbeer's plan of writing alternative scorings in differently coloured inks to find how they sounded was a favourite subject of derision with Elgar. He could not understand the need for any experiments in orchestration. Nothing in his own work ever surprised him when he heard it coming from the orchestra, or choir and orchestra, for the first time: he just *knew* how it would sound, and was never disappointed.

He would very rarely talk about the actual technique of writing. He was perfectly sincere and literal when he said, speaking of a well-known ex-musical critic, "He knows more about music than I do," and, of an equally prominent teacher and composer, " I

149

cannot talk to him about music." I have already described how, on my first approach to him with a request for professional instruction in harmony and counterpoint, he put me off with " My dear boy, I don't know anything about these things." Once, as we came out of Lincoln Cathedral after a performance of *Gerontius*, he said, rubbing his hands gleefully, "Billy, I believe there is a lot of double counterpoint, or whatever they call it, in that." He spoke as though he had only just discovered it, and " or whatever they call it " was to me a very subtle illumination of what was really at the back of his mind in talking of these matters. Needless to say, his knowledge in this direction was unassailable, and, though he was a little whimsical about it and would never let himself go— for fear, I always think, of being thought academic— nothing escaped him. He kept himself well informed as to the musical output of his contemporaries, studying and listening to the works of the most modern of them. He did not love them very much, but they interested him, and I never heard him abuse any of them, or say an unkind word about the most bizarre or outrageous of their efforts. How easily he understood them musically was shown on more than one occasion by the few remarks or observations he let fall in our conversations.

None of these things influenced him at all in his own musical conception: they only entertained him. As will be seen by a study of the fragments he left of his Third Symphony, he went on progressing as he grew older, but writing, as ever, entirely in his own way.

I think that it was his general and vast knowledge of the world around him that lay behind his facility in expressing himself musically, in addition, of course, to his innate æsthetic sense, his acutely sensitive nature, his wisdom and mature judgment.

He went about the world from his earliest youth with eyes to see, and ears to hear; and I am sure not very much that was going on anywhere escaped him. He seemed to me to know a great deal about architecture—very much more than I, at all events—with all the technical names, the dates of the different styles, and the peculiarities of the ancient tombs which we used to go into the churches to see for ourselves. He would tell me all about them in the most interesting manner; and he was never at a loss for an answer to any of my questions when I developed a thirst for knowledge of this sort while walking round with him at Warwick Castle, the church at Cropthorne (where there are some remarkable tombs), in Lincoln or Canterbury Cathedrals, or at the Madeleine or Notre-Dame in Paris. He was always an informative guide in such places.

He had great literary knowledge too, and an omnivorous taste for it. He knew all the great poets; he loved and adored every word of Shakespeare; and he read all the modern writers of poetry with interest.

151

He liked some light reading, but not very much; but he was very amused always with the works of O. Henry, one of whose books was generally by his bedside.

He retained a convenient stock of legal knowledge from the days when he was a boy in a lawyer's office. He was curious about science, and was by no means merely playing with his microscopes and his studies of practical and theoretical chemistry in his own laboratory at Hereford. He was always interested in history, and had a memory for dates and happenings which was quite prodigious. Theology also was a great topic when I first knew him. He could hold his own in any discussion, as can be very well understood when we consider that he must have known his Bible from end to end to have compiled the libretto for *The Apostles* and *The Kingdom*, and prepared the third part, which he never set to music. Every word in these libretti is taken from the Scriptures. As this must have been a simple operation of memory and not of the drudgery of research work, it may be taken as a proof of his exceptional mental power; for if the ready command of all the passages, and the extraordinary ingenuity displayed in their selection and arrangement to carry the story on logically throughout the oratorios, had been as difficult for him as for an ordinary mortal, he would never have dreamt of undertaking it. As it was, he never dreamt of handing it over to the nearest clergyman, but he would

PLATE XIII : THE ELGAR CHILDREN IN 1868

(EDWARD IS SEATED; HIS BROTHER FRANK STANDING NEXT TO HIM. BEHIND THE
TABLE ON THE LEFT IS POLLY (MRS. GRAFTON), ON THE RIGHT LUCY, AND SEATED
IN FRONT IS " DOT " (HELEN)

discuss the theological aspect, and explain his own views to his friends Canon Gorton or Dean Armitage Robinson.

To try to sum up the characteristics of Elgar as a musician, without reference to his completeness as a man, is impossible; his subjects were so varied and his art so versatile. He trod all musical paths that led to artistic ends, whether this should end in a small piece for violin and piano, a national patriotic song, or a symphony or oratorio. One thing is common to all his works great or small, and that is the stamp of a powerful personality, patent to anyone who listens to a few bars taken anywhere at random from any of his works.

In spite of the spiritual mysticism inherent in his mind, he started his excursions always with his feet on the ground. The Enigma Variations began with real people. I have sometimes had a day-dream of a concert at which each variation was followed by the appearance on the platform of the dedicatee, so that the audience might compare the Elgar transfiguration with the sitter. The transfiguration was always a spiritualisation; but it was gathered from the commonplace facts of life. The late Mr. Jaeger of Novellos' (Nimrod) was well known to many of the other living British composers; but only Elgar thought of getting immortal music out of him. The variation labelled with three asterisks sets us asking, " Who was this ? Is it someone who died ? " It leaves one wondering and creates the atmosphere of mysticism which was natural to Elgar.

The phrases and quotations written on the MSS. of his works, even the things he wrote in people's books—one hopes these are all being carefully preserved by their various owners—are all throbs of his own life. In my copy of *The Music Makers* he has written, " 'Musicians thinke our Soules are harmonies' (Sr. Jno. Davies)." Upon the Violin Concerto he has inscribed a Spanish saying:

"Aqui esta encerrada el alma de........, 1910."
(Herein is inscribed the soul of . . . . . .)

The original autograph full score of *The Dream of Gerontius* has the following in his own handwriting just after the last double bar:

" This is the best of me; for the rest, I ate, and drank, and slept, and loved and hated, like another: my life was as the vapour, and is not; but *this* I saw and knew; this, if anything of mine, is worth your memory.
" EDWARD ELGAR,
" Birchwood Lodge,
" *August* 13*th*, 1900."

On the printed version of the score he has written, " Birchwood. In Summer, 1900." He made all who took part in the first performance at Birmingham on

October 3rd, 1900, sign the score, amongst them being
Hans Richter, who added this strange stanza:

> *" Let drop the Chorus.*
> *Let drop everybody!*
> *but let* NOT *drop the*
> *wings of your original*
> *genius.*
>
> " HANS RICHTER."

To those who remember the thick, almost guttural,
timbre of Richter's voice, it does not need much
imagination to hear him roll this out, full-throated
and with great sonority. I have many of these sayings
of Hans Richter still echoing in my head, and can
still distinctly hear him delivering himself of the above
lines, every inflection of his voice being clear and
distinct in my memory.

Elgar's desk and writing-table were always a source
of great interest to me. I was fascinated by his sheaf of
pencils, all beautifully sharpened ready for instant use,
his pens arranged by the inkstand, and a raw potato
in the place of honour in the centre.

This potato was used to clean his pen. If it got in
the least clogged it was at once plunged into the
potato and withdrawn quite clean. I asked him why
he used steel pens when he had many fountain-pens
which had been presented to him from time to time.
His reply was, " I use a steel pen so that I shall have
to keep going forward to dip it in the ink, instead of
keeping my hand in the same position the whole time,

you old owl! Do you think I want to get writer's cramp—a thing I have never suffered from?"

His varied assortment of sealing-wax and his fine collection of seals were also of great interest. He loved seals, and had made one or two himself: one was made of quite a good-sized piece of metal on which he had punched the letters E. E. deeply, so that they made a bold impression. The wax was of all colours, his favourite being a deep blue; he loved sealing his things with this, however unnecessarily.

Paper-cutters, clips, clothes-pegs to clip loose papers, magnifying glass, calendar, blotters large and small— these were all there; and there was an enormous waste-paper basket at his side, ready for the debris of his morning's post.

He used music-paper ruled on one side only; so that, if he made a blot or spoiled anything he was writing, he could take a clean sheet and there was " only one page to copy instead of two."

This was his environment. Here he would sit hour after hour scoring his works, his piano a little way off in case he wanted to try anything he had written and give his hand a rest; then back to his desk, his old steel pen scratching away and flying over the paper to an accompaniment of growls and exclamations when he made a smudge or put a note on the wrong line. It is very difficult to think that he sits there no more, but comforting to know that what he set down at that desk, the fruit of his inspiration, of the genius that crystallised and caught from life every mood and shade of meaning and fixed it in music for all time, this is ours for ever.

Before leaving him thus, let us still picture him sitting there writing that infinite tune which has no beginning and no end. The passage is on p. 184 in the vocal score of *The Kingdom*, at the end of the setting of the Lord's Prayer; and the words are "For ever and ever. Amen."

In thinking of Elgar primarily as a composer, one is inclined, however, to overlook his talents and natural facility as a conductor, especially as an interpreter of his own works.

How often is it the case that a composer is by no means the best or the most competent to undertake this task!

Richard Wagner was a professional conductor of many years' experience, and could produce an atmosphere—in *Die Walküre* or *Tristan*, for instance—that has hardly been reproduced since; but, when he conducted at the Wagner Festivals at the Albert Hall, the orchestra always shamelessly showed their relief by applauding loudly when his place was taken half way through the concert by the more composed and helpful young Hans Richter, who then laid the foundation of his English fame as a conductor.

There is a story, too, which I have heard told many times, concerning Dvořák and his visit to an English festival to conduct the first performance of his *Stabat Mater*. On the day of his expected arrival the following telegram came: " Please send one to snatch me from the train lest I should not recognise the journey." He was duly snatched from the train, and conducted his rehearsals quite ably and normally; but at the performance he became very absorbed and meditative; so much so that during one of the movements his beat got more and more absent-minded, the music meanwhile dragging painfully and becoming slower and slower.

It became quite evident that the conductor's attention had completely wandered from the performance. He was apparently back in his study examining with interest the lay-out of the score or mentally transposing the horns in E or F to their actual sounds. At any rate, he was quite oblivious of the imminence of disaster. As the music showed signs of coming to a complete standstill, the leader of the orchestra deemed some desperate remedy to be essential; so he screwed up his courage and, leaning forward, brought Dvořák back to earth by a smart dig in the ribs with the point of his bow.

This considerably astonished the composer-conductor; but it produced the desired effect, and the situation was saved.

In speaking of Elgar as a conductor, the fact has to be recorded that the very finest performances of his works have taken place under his own baton. Any one of the choristers, soloists, or players who took part in any of his oratorios, especially in the performances given in the cathedrals of the Three Choirs, will unhesitatingly corroborate this statement.

He had something quite magnetic about him when he took his place at the conductor's desk. He had the power to hold everyone with his glance; and when his sensitive hands—with those long, delicate fingers— were raised, the atmosphere was tense, the mood established.

Without effort he conveyed all his meaning, and obtained the desired result. He had the very rare gift of showing his inmost feelings by his facial expression, his quick, almost nervous gestures. His own early experience as an orchestral player had taught him the most valuable lesson: *he allowed the orchestra to play.*

Many conductors imagine that their art is enhanced by a continual display of what they imagine to be mastery over the unfortunate players, flogging them onward or dramatically holding them up, impeding and harrying their performance at every point, in the fond belief that thus they are thereby giving a profound (or otherwise) reading of the work they essay to conduct. What is it to them if ten or twenty notes lie inside a beat? If they are feeling impetuous, they lash about regardless of the fact that the players have to rush their notes to catch the next beat. If the performance is consequently untidy, the orchestra is of course to blame.

Other conductors put their orchestras into a sort of mental strait-waistcoat. Every string player must use precisely the same amount of bow, exactly in the same spot, mapped out with an imaginary foot-rule. Every wind instrumentalist must alter completely any sort of preconceived idea he may have had as to the phrasing, tone colour, or interpretation of any solo passage. Nobody has a single bar, from one end of the work to the other, in which he is free to let himself go; in fact, to play his instrument. He is always checking his natural expression, stifling his tone, and playing with extreme discomfort. He is not surprised to read in the Press the next morning that "Mr. Blank had his forces well in hand and secured a particularly neat and clean performance of the work." He puts down the paper knowing full well that the said performance lacked everything that really mattered: life, blood, spontaneity, spirituality, everything—it was as dead as mutton.

Elgar knew all this: he allowed the band to play; he obtained fire, passion, serenity, and, above all, spirituality, often when his expressive hands hardly moved.

It was a memorable experience to play under him. How his eyes roved from one instrument to another ! How they lit up when one of his pet phrases or passages arrived ! How he used to fix me with his eyes with a tense expression which said, "Listen to those trumpets," or, "Listen to the trombones," as he nodded his head in their direction.

The joy, too, that suffused his face when the side-drum did his little tap by himself in *Falstaff*. On every page something came to light up his expression and stir his never flagging enthusiasm. Is it any wonder that all this intense feeling he himself felt for every bar of the music] should be infectious, and that it should be caught by the players and singers under him, and imparted unfailingly and faithfully to the listeners ?

No need to flog the orchestra with superhuman gestures and wild efforts to rouse them. They had only to look on his face, and they gave him everything that they had, to the last ounce.

Elgar as the conductor of music by other composers was not so successful. He was naturally very diffident and restrained in dealing with anyone's work but his own; and this hampered him in many ways, so that he could not obtain that spontaneous expression that he nearly always elicited for his own works.

When he accepted the position of conductor-in-chief at one of the series of symphony concerts given by the London Symphony Orchestra soon after the war, he always gave me the impression that he was a little nervous and rather undecided in his interpretations; but he certainly had great moments when he forgot himself and threw himself heart and soul into the performance.

When he conducted the Harrison tour in 1916 he became very sure of himself as the tour progressed, and he conducted the same works night after night in each town. I remember specially a most impressive performance of Brahms's Third Symphony, which he adored. Also he accompanied Arthur de Greef most sympathetically in the Piano Concerto in G minor by Saint-Saëns, also in a fantasia on *Melodies Flamandes* (or some title very much like that) by de Greef himself. In the last movement of the latter work the composer, who was himself the soloist, had a curious way of moving his whole body to the rhythm and of throwing up his hands at the ends of the phrases, so that after a few performances this work came to be renamed by the orchestra and was known as " The Dancing Flamingo." De Greef never knew this; but we told Elgar, and he used to bite his lip every night as he opened the score and saw the title, trying to keep a straight face in spite of his own strong sense of humour. This became more difficult at each repetition; and as we approached the last movement his facial expression, which he strove vainly to control, broke down, his hand stole over the lower half of his face, concealing his twitching mouth, and his eyes roved round in our direction, saying quite distinctly, " You wretches ! "

Now that Elgar has gone from us and we can no longer play his works under his own inspiring direction, how fortunate we are that our contemporary conductors regard his great works from the right angle, taking infinite care over the performances and doing

PLATE XIV: "LIKE SOMETHING WE HEAR DOWN BY THE RIVER"

their utmost to perpetuate the tradition Elgar himself established.

One feels bound, in this connection, to single out Sir Landon Ronald. Sir Landon has at all times devoted his great gifts to the interpretation of Elgar's music. I have heard it said that when he was listening to Elgar conducting a rehearsal, he had great difficulty in restraining himself from rushing on to the platform and taking the baton from Elgar's hand, such was the almost over-mastering desire he experienced to conduct the works he loves so well. One must also admire the extraordinary clarity of his mind in seeing, or rather hearing, in an instant what is amiss at a rehearsal, and putting his finger unerringly on the spot in a most practical manner.

It is a great comfort to all Elgarians who were wont to flock to the cathedrals and concert-rooms to see the great man conduct his own works, to know that they still have conductors deeply imbued with the Elgar spirit and tradition; a tradition which is being carried on too by the younger school of conductors, who, let us hope, will pass it on to those who come after, so that a real understanding of this music and all it stands and has stood for will be perpetuated. How true it is that a composer is completely at the mercy of his interpreters! If an artist paints a picture, he can hang it up for all to see. No one seeks to "touch it up," or put some more into it, or work off any of his own idiosyncrasies through it. There it is, a permanent

record of the artist's thought and the genius by which
he succeeded in getting it on to the canvas. But when
a composer has registered his thought, however skil-
fully, on a paper score in black and white, his music
is still inaudible and unreadable by the great majority.
It has to wait for the executants, conductors, orchestral players, soloists, and choristers to bring to life the
symbols inscribed upon the paper.

The consideration of this responsibility should
surely give pause to those who from sheer egotism
wish to impose their own personality upon every piece
of music they interpret. I remember a very noted
prima donna at Covent Garden Opera House who was
the proud possessor of one or two superlatively good
notes in the upper register of her voice. On arriving
at one of these notes, nothing would induce her to
relinquish her hold on it while she had breath. This,
unfortunately for her, occurred once when Hans
Richter was conducting a rehearsal of *Fidelio*. Upon
arriving at the longed-for note the prima donna
indulged in a long-drawn pause, holding it on with
beautiful quality and a seraphic facial expression,
which rapidly changed to one of extreme annoyance
when she saw the orchestra and the conductor going
on with the succeeding bars, leaving her high and dry
on her lovely note. Swallowing her rage, she advanced
to the footlights and said, " Oh, Dr. Richter, I make a
pause there on that G." " A pause," said Richter;
" there is no pause." " Oh, no, I know there is no

pause marked in the music; but *I* make one there."
" There is no pause," again said Richter, as he looked
more closely into the score. " Oh, I know that,"
reiterated the good lady, losing her temper a little;
" but I tell you I make one there." In slow and very
measured tones, Richter said, " If Beethove' had wish
a pause, he would have mark. He have *not* mark, so
we do not make." The rehearsal proceeded.

Elgar as a conductor was particularly careful to
carry out every authentic mark introduced by the
composer, and always set his face against the smallest
alteration or cut introduced by anyone in a serious
work. Never did he seek to impose anything of his own
personality to detract from the composer's evident
intention. It is to be hoped that posterity will deal as
faithfully with his own works.

PART III

THE THIRD SYMPHONY

THE THIRD SYMPHONY

BEFORE ENTERING upon the description of this work, let me quote a letter I received from Bernard Shaw, which may act as an additional deterrent to anyone who may think that, after all, it is a tragedy that this symphony should remain unperformed, and that some other composer should take its fragments and build them into some sort of practicable coherency: in short, as Elgar said, tinker with it.

"17th August, 1934.

"What is a symphony? A hundred years ago it was a composition in a clear symmetrical pattern established by Haydn and called Sonata Form. Now if half a symmetrical design is completed, any draughtsman can supply the missing half. If Haydn had died during the composition of one of his symphonies, and had left notes of its themes, and a hint or two of its bridge passages, Beethoven could easily have contributed a perfect Haydn symphony from them as an act of piety or a musical *jeu d'esprit*.

"On the same terms any educated musician could construct an unfinished Rossini overture.

169

" But no composer of symphonies nowadays adheres to the decorative patterns. The musical romances and extravaganzas of Berlioz, the symphonic poems of Liszt and Strauss, and the tone-dramas of Wagner could not have conformed to symmetrical decorative patterns : they had to find expressionist forms : and to reconstruct a lost expressionist composition from a fragment would be as impossible as to reconstruct a Shakespeare sonnet from the first two lines of it.

" All the great symphonies after Beethoven are as expressionist as Wagner's music-dramas, even when, as in the Symphonies of Brahms and Elgar, the skeleton of the old pattern is still discernible. All possibility of reconstruction from fragments or completion from beginnings is gone.

" Consequently, though Elgar left some sketches of a third symphony and was actually at work on it when he died, no completion or reconstruction is possible : the symphony, like Beethoven's tenth, died with the composer."

The material for a third symphony had been in Elgar's mind for years. Some of the themes and ideas are written down in his scrap-books, in various guises—frequently the same phrase repeated in different keys. In the latter part of 1933 he began to get all these fragments—in some instances as many as twenty or thirty consecutive bars—on paper, though they were rarely harmonically complete. A clear vision of the whole symphony was forming in his mind. He would write a portion of the Finale, or the middle section of the second movement, and then work at the development of the first movement. It did not seem at all odd to him to begin things in the middle, or to switch off suddenly from one movement to another. It is evident that he had the whole conception in his head in a more or less nebulous condition. He told me that it was not going to be cast in the same form as the two earlier symphonies, but was to be simpler in construction and design. He was going to revert to the old-fashioned repeat in the exposition of the first movement with a *prima* and *seconda volta*. The second movement was to be of a light character with contrasts, but not quick: it was to be a slow-moving kind of Scherzo.

Of the slow movement, he wrote the main themes out on a single stave for me to play them on the violin while he filled in the harmonies on the piano. (This he did also to the whole of the exposition of the first movement and to fragments and portions of the others.) One day we played a great deal of it in this manner—i.e. violin and piano—to Mr. and Mrs. Bernard Shaw when they came to Marl Bank to tea. The last movement was to be fiery and rugged; but I never could find out how it was to end. Whenever I asked the question he always became mysterious and vague, and said, " Ah, that we shall see," or something non-committal; and I could not induce him to begin the slow movement at the beginning. We always started either at the middle section or what I imagined would be about the sixth or eighth bar.

I have been through reams of MSS. to find any scraps or fragments that have any bearing on this work; and they are now all collected and sorted into the various movements; but how nebulous it is, how woefully lacking in cohesion, can be seen by those who can induce the B.B.C. to let them see the MSS., which are now their property in safe keeping at Broadcasting House. For the benefit of those who cannot go there to see it for themselves, I will try to describe the symphony in detail and endeavour to bridge some of the gulfs which make it very incoherent in places by describing as nearly as I can remember what he told me he was going to do, but was not spared to write down.

First Movement—Allegro Molto Maestoso

Without any preliminary preparation or introductory matter we plunge at once into a definite statement of the principal subject: a theme of rugged and sweeping character in 12-8 time—music which sounds as though it had always been going on, as the sound of the sea, or the wind in the trees—inevitable music. The key, in spite of the three flats in the signature, is somewhat indefinite, the fifths in contrary motion and

PLATE XV : ELGAR WITH HIS BROTHER FRANK AT WORCESTER CATHEDRAL

the accidentals in the very first bar producing this restless tonality. If we play over the first two bars once or twice, however, it will be found that the impression left upon the mind is distinctly C major, and it is not until the ninth and tenth bars are reached that there is any sensation of C minor. The rhythmic structure is very persistent, also the theme is practically written in canon, the bass following the treble at a distance of two beats, until it is unexpectedly and abruptly stopped short in its headlong career at the eighth bar, by the appearance of the chord of B♭ minor on the second beat of the bar marked *fortissimo* and *sforzando*.

This is all that is finished in the full score of this section, i.e. two pages of four bars each (*Example* 1). There are fifteen more pages ruled with the bar lines and the notes written for one instrument, just forming a thread to carry the bars up to pp. 17, 18, and 19, where the end of the Exposition is indicated with its *Prima* and *Seconda Volta* (*Ex.* 2a). Fortunately, in the sketch, which is written in short score, we can see the structure and treatment of the rest of this section (*Ex.* 2b, i–vi). After two bars based upon the opening theme, we meet the companion in the lower instruments, a strong and very definite piece of writing in C minor, with a decorative accompaniment written above and evidently meant for the violin and upper wood-wind. This continues to swing along until at the twenty-seventh bar we have a change of time signature to Common time, and the second subject is announced in E♭ major.

This is a warm and singing melody very much in the Elgarian manner, having the characteristic dotted crotchet followed by a quaver (*legato* and *cantabile*) repeated for many bars, as in both the other symphonies and in many of his earlier works. In this case the figuration persists for thirteen bars before it is modified by the appearance of the even crotchets (on the first half of the bar and then on the second half). Soon we meet the companion theme to the earlier part of the second subject in E♭ major. It is written in a broad and expressive manner (the composer has written *largo* over it) passing through various keys and bringing us eventually and very naturally to the double bar and the repeat, which he so expressly indicates.

One can but wonder what sort of justice the present-day interpreters of the classics imagine they are doing to the composers whose works they essay when they carefully omit every repeat except, perhaps, those directed to be made in the menuet and trio (with the *da capo*)—repeats which are only retained, one imagines, because the sections are usually short. At any rate, Elgar had the repeat of this exposition very positively in his mind, and the shape and balance of the first movement were dependent upon the observance of his direction. Also, as can be seen by examining *Exs.* 3*a* and 3*b*, much time and care went to the fashioning of this ingenious passage both in the bowing, which I had to play countless times in every conceivable manner, and also in the rearrangement of the first violins *divisi*, so that they mount in minor seconds from the note G through two octaves to the high G which concludes the Exposition.

After the repeat this is again used in the *Seconda Volta* (*Ex.* 3*c*), and we have a mere three bars added to form an idea as to how the development would proceed. There are, however, a few bars more or less completed in short score to guide us. After a page (*Ex.* 4) on which is written " leading to *réprise*," dealing with material derived from the principal subject and giving some idea as to how the development section will end, we are confronted with another gap. No indication is given as to how the *réprise* was to be worked, whether it was to be a repetition of the material in the exposition, amplified, or modified, or perhaps a little further developed. We can only conjecture.

The next definite piece of MS. has " After the *réprise*, leading to second appearance of the Second Subject " inscribed upon it. This shows the change of key signature to C major (*Ex.* 5*a*) and the reappearance of the Second Subject which is continued through another whole page (*Ex.* 5*b*). Another fragment (*Ex.* 6) occurs somewhere towards the end, and *Ex.* 7 is all we have to show that he was dealing with the first and second subjects (now brought very close together)

175

before actually entering upon the Coda. This he has marked " near the end " all too prophetically.

There are two more pages of full score (*Exs. 8a* and *8b*) (completed as can be seen by the insertion of rests in all the empty bars), and these bars are evidently fragments from the development section, but it is difficult to decide where they actually fit when so much is unwritten.

Second Movement—Allegretto

The second movement is described on many pages of the short score as " Scherzo," but on the very first page he has written " in place of Scherzo Sym. III " (*Ex. 9a*); he wrote this out again with an additional bar of introduction (*Ex. 9b*). He must have had the main theme for this movement (very light and rather wistful) in his mind for some years, as I have seen it scribbled in his scrap books in various forms when looking through, on occasions, in my endeavour to trace any pieces having any bearing upon this symphony. He loved this simple little theme, and we played it again and again with violin and piano.

There is nothing to indicate what followed, but, as far as I can remember, we used to go on to the new subject, or episode (*Ex. 10*), without a break, then return to the first subject with slightly different treatment, then to the next episode (*Ex. 11*). He could not make up his mind, apparently, what key he wanted, as can be seen by the query at the top of the page, also by the fact that the following page (*Ex.* 12), which indicates the next return to the first subject is written in three flats—rather a problem to anyone trying to piece these fragments together. *Ex.* 13 also implies modulation or trial of key, and the last example (with another query at the top of the page as to the key) shows exactly how this movement ends (*Ex.* 14).

Third Movement—Adagio

The third movement was originally begun in E♭ major, but was later written in D (*Exs.* 15*a* and 15*b*). The only part of this movement which is complete is this broad, dignified, and very expressive melody of eighteen bars which we played from a violin part that he wrote out for me. He exhorted me to " tear my heart out " each time we repeated it, so much was he always overcome by its emotional significance. I was never able to induce him to write down the continuation, but I was allowed to play a bar or two (looking over his shoulder) from the fragments on one or two other scraps of MSS. (*Exs.* 16*a* and 16*b*), but I could never prevail upon him to divulge in what order they were to appear.

Last Movement—Finale

The last movement opens majestically with an introductory four bars in full score (*Ex.* 17*a*), followed by an Allegro of turbulent character, as can be seen in *Ex.* 17*b* at the place marked " begin " in the composer's handwriting. After some more bars, which he used to play with great vigour and excitement on the piano, he would say, " Now, let into this as hard as you can " (*Exs.* 18*a* and 18*b*). Then, at the *dim.*, we glided into the companion theme at the change of key to three naturals. The short score with the harmony for this subject is to be seen in *Ex.* 18*c*. Two pages having some relationship to one another evidently follow on here in some way (*Exs.* 19*a* and 19*b*), the *Nobilmente* phrase in two flats in *Ex.* 19*b* being treated in augmentation at the *piu lento* in *Ex.* 19*a*, but it is difficult to decide exactly where, or in what part of the movement, they should be placed.

The next fragment (*Ex.* 20) concludes the exposition, though what that pedal B♭ *sf* leads to is unfortunately not written. There is a new version of the companion theme to the first subject (*Ex.* 18*c*) which appears now with a signature of three flats (*Ex.* 21), and which is probably intended to appear as contrast to something very exciting in the development section or towards the end. Another page (*Ex.* 22), which is in the nature of a peroration, looks as though it were leading up energetically to the final Coda, but this is mere conjecture, as there is nothing to show this; obviously it is derived from the fragments seen in *Exs.* 19*a* and 19*b*.

Alas ! that there is no Coda to be found—he never played anything to show in what manner it should end, not even improvisation, but would leave off suddenly and abruptly when we arrived anywhere near that part, and say, " Enough of this ; let us go out and take the dogs on the Common." Also, he would be very restless and ill at ease, and would not discuss the symphony any more, and it would be quite a while before he became calm and resumed his normal good spirits. Then his last terrible illness began, and so there was no more writing or playing until one day, not very long before he left us, he wrote in pencil, as he lay in his bed, this last example (*Ex.* 23), probably the very last notes he put upon paper, and which he kept by him to show me on my next visit to his bedside. He would not say whether it was the end of the slow movement Adagio, or the end of the whole symphony. All he said (with tears streaming down his cheeks) was—" Billy, this is the end."

PART IV

THE THIRD SYMPHONY
FACSIMILES

EXAMPLE 1   182

EXAMPLE I

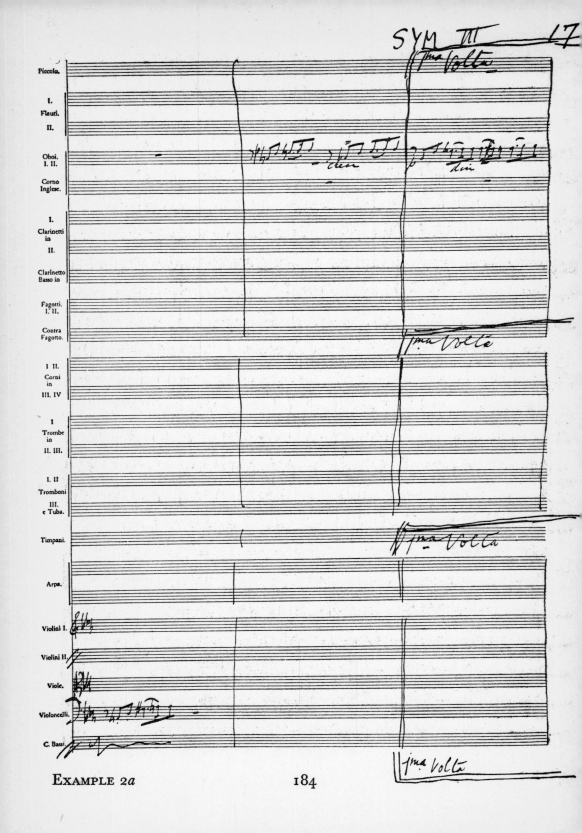

EXAMPLE 2a

185

EXAMPLE 2*b* (i)

EXAMPLE 2*b* (ii)

EXAMPLE 2*b* (iii)

EXAMPLE 2*b* (iv)

EXAMPLE 2*b* (v)

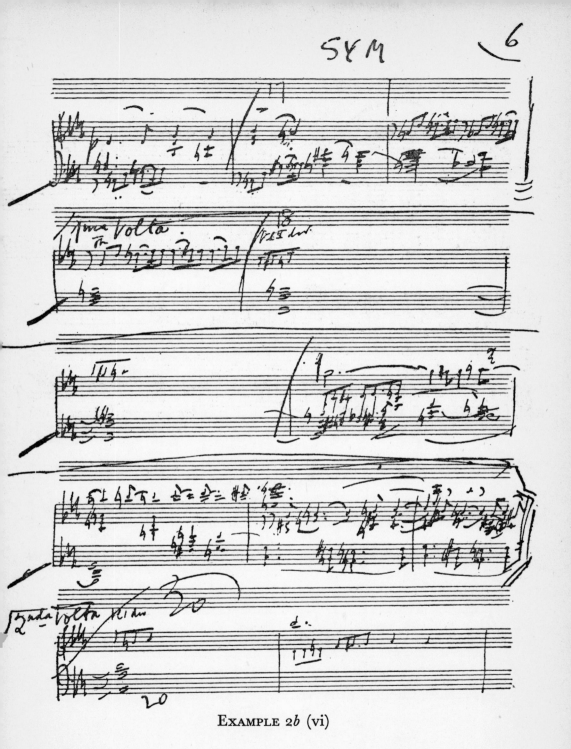

Example 2*b* (vi)

EXAMPLE 3a

EXAMPLE 3*b*

EXAMPLE 3c

EXAMPLE 4

195

EXAMPLE 5a

EXAMPLE 5*b*

EXAMPLE 6

SYM. III

near the end

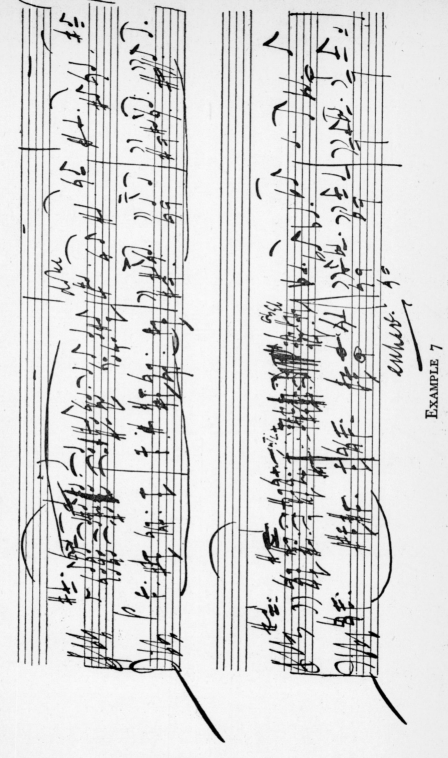

EXAMPLE 7

199

EXAMPLE 8a

200

201   EXAMPLE 8*b*

EXAMPLE 9a

EXAMPLE 9b

EXAMPLE 10

EXAMPLE II

EXAMPLE 12

EXAMPLE 13

EXAMPLE 14

Example 15*a*

EXAMPLE 15*b*

EXAMPLE 16a

211

EXAMPLE 16*b*

Example 17a

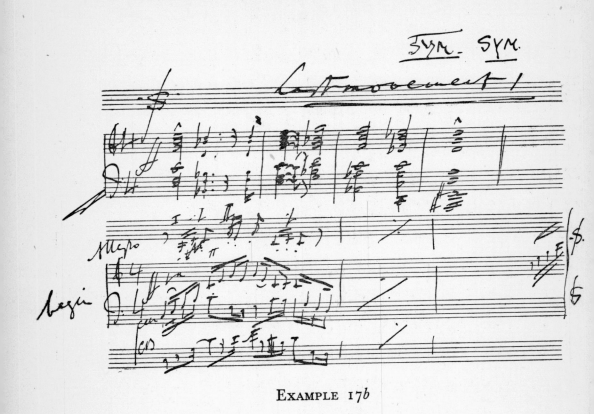

EXAMPLE 17*b*

FINALE

EXAMPLE 18a

215

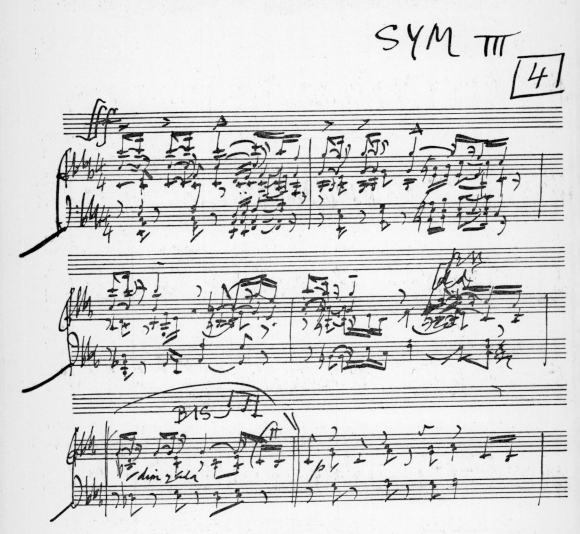

EXAMPLE 18*b*

EXAMPLE 18c

EXAMPLE 19*a*

EXAMPLE 19*b*

EXAMPLE 20

EXAMPLE 21

EXAMPLE 22

EXAMPLE 23